A MIDWIFE IN MY POCKET

Pregnancy, Birth,
and Life with a
New Baby, Told as
It Really Is

EMMA COOK

authorHOUSE®

AuthorHouse™ UK
1663 Liberty Drive
Bloomington, IN 47403 USA
www.authorhouse.co.uk
Phone: 0800.197.4150

Published by AuthorHouse 11/16/2016

ISBN: 978-1-5246-6510-4 (sc)
ISBN: 978-1-5246-6509-8 (hc)
ISBN: 978-1-5246-6632-3 (e)

*I would like to dedicate this book to all the families
I have worked with during my career, and to all the babies
I have had the privilege to help into this world.*

*Some of you have made me smile,
and some of you have made me shed a tear.*

*You are all very special, and I would like to thank you all,
along with my amazing son and family who have put
up with me whilst I have been writing this book.*

Em Cook x

Contents

Introduction

I have the best job in the world – no honestly. I get up every morning and look forward to what my day will bring.

So for all the happy times you have all given me, along with some sad times, I am writing this book for you, the parent-to-be or new parent.

I want it to be different to other books. There are loads of books out there for new parents, but this one is a very practical (hopefully user friendly) guide to help you through your journey.

I want it to become your best friend and hold your hand at this incredible time of your life. Use it, cherish it, and above all enjoy it.

I am writing this because I have been working with pregnant Mums and new families for nearly 20 years now. So that's what I do, what I live for – I am a Midwife.

As well as being a Midwife (mainly in the community), I am a Mum. I remember bringing my brand new baby home from the hospital (I had qualified and worked as a Midwife for 8 years when he was born), and to be honest I was terrified.

You do everything you can to protect your baby during pregnancy – a sort of protective shell around him or her. Then suddenly the world seems a scary place. If it was like that for me, then I often wonder what it is like for a complete novice.

Our society has changed from extended families that meant we were around babies all of the time and child rearing was second nature. We had our close family living either in the same house, or very close. Now because of the pressures of life we are more isolated, often with little or no experience of a newborn baby and their demands (and believe me, they do demand!)

Couple this with all of the adverts we are bombarded with, showing sunlight streaming through windows and babies sleeping peacefully all in white, whilst the Mum looks fresh faced, slim and stunning.

Did anyone tell you it's not like this? Maybe not, as in my experience parenthood is a shock – even to those Mums who have had a baby before. Even to us new Mums who are midwives and think we should know what it's really like.

Did you know that you still look pregnant for a good few weeks after the baby is born? No – I thought not.

Life is not like the A-list celebs make out. It can be challenging.

If I had a pound for every first visit I have done, where the new Mum feels as though it's all too much, then I would be a very rich woman!

So let's tell the truth – what is pregnancy and early parenthood REALLY like?

What are the important things to remember throughout your pregnancy?

What things do you REALLY need for a new baby?

What tips can I give you that will make life calmer?

I must stress, this is not designed to be a medical book. There will be tips about what to look out for in pregnancy and the early postnatal period. This book is designed so that it strips back all of the other books – which means that you can focus on what is important to you. If you need more in depth information, then you can refer to other books that contain more medical detail.

This is the first book I have written, and it has taken me a fair few years to pluck up the courage to do this. However, every day I see courageous people doing amazing things, and if I can make just one person less stressed and more confident, then this book will have done its' job.

As a Midwife I feel as though I am helping newly emerged butterflies, who need to dry their wings to enable themselves to fly.

I provide the warm breeze of my knowledge and training to give newly pregnant Mums the confidence to embrace this new experience, and move forward on their journey to flight.

This is what I do. Hold your hand as long as is needed and then take great pride in the fact that all of a sudden you don't need me. You have grown your wings and you can fly. This is what makes my job so humbling and a complete privilege.

So as you are all brave beyond belief, then so will I be by writing this book.

Chapter One

'I'm Pregnant!'

So you've planned a baby, or maybe found out you are pregnant and it wasn't exactly on the 'to do' list.

What on earth do you do?

Firstly you don't need to do loads of pregnancy tests...... If it's positive, then you ARE pregnant. The hormones that tell the test you are pregnant are only there in pregnancy.

Then probably the first thing would be to book an appointment to see your GP. This is a good idea, but not essential anymore. It may be an idea to contact your local maternity unit and find out if they have a self-referral system.

TOP TIP! Wait until you are about 6 weeks before self-referring, and if you think you are further on, then do it as soon as possible. Ideally most hospitals would like to see you before 10 weeks to discuss early screening options and take certain blood tests, which your Midwife will explain to you.

Are you taking folic acid? If not, take it as soon as you have a positive pregnancy test. This is really important for your developing baby as it helps the baby's spine develop and reduces the risk of the baby having problems later on, such as Spina Bifida. However folic acid is part of our daily diet, so don't panic. Just start it as soon as possible when you find out.

The Department of Health (at the time of writing this book) recommends women take 400mcgs of folic acid once a day as soon as they are planning to conceive (or as soon as possible after the pregnancy is confirmed – if a little bit of a surprise), until 12 weeks.

If you or your partner have a family history of problems such as Spina Bifida, or have had a previous child affected by it, then you will need to see your GP as you'll need a higher dose of folic acid (5mg). This also includes diabetic and epileptic women too. If you have ANY doubt, then contact your GP or talk to your Midwife.

Folic acid won't do any harm if taken after 12 weeks if you aren't sure of your dates, it just won't be as useful as the baby's spine will be fully developed.

TOP TIP! *Only stop taking your folic acid after you have had your dates confirmed at your 12 week scan – then you know for sure you are past this important stage in your baby's life. This is really important, and should not be confused with multi-vitamin supplements.*

TOP TIP! *A pregnancy multi vitamin supplement can be taken for the whole of your pregnancy. However there have been recent reports in the news at the time of writing this book to say that vitamins have been found to be less useful than originally thought.*

<u>Please don't take a vitamin supplement that isn't formulated for pregnancy. Vitamin A is not recommended and too much could harm your baby.</u>

DID YOU KNOW? *Vitamin D is really important too? Vitamin D helps the baby's bones and teeth develop to become nice and strong. The recommended dose (at the time of writing this book) is 10mcg per day for the whole of your pregnancy, and as with folic acid, should be taken as early as possible in your pregnancy.*

TOP TIP! *Avoid herbal remedies as there has not been enough research done to ensure their safety yet.*

TOP TIP! *Always check with a pharmacist that the over the counter medicines which you wish to purchase are safe to take in pregnancy.*

To try and avoid low iron levels, as well as taking your pregnancy vitamin supplements every day, there are other easy ways to make sure your body is absorbing iron well.......

TOP TIP! *Drinks containing vitamin C, such as fruit juices are good with each main meal as they help your body absorb the iron in your food more easily. Try and avoid milky / caffeine drinks within an hour of eating a main meal as this can make your body less efficient at processing the iron in your food.*

Read up about good foods to eat in pregnancy, especially if you are a Vegetarian or Vegan.

Also some foods aren't great in pregnancy, so make sure you do your research. <u>The main ones to avoid are</u>:

Pate

Liver

Blue-veined cheeses

Soft cheeses, such as Brie and Camembert

Eat no more than 4 cans of tuna a week or 2 tuna steaks or 2 portions of oily fish

Thick-shakes (the type served in fast-food places)

Soft whippy ice cream

TOP TIP! Eat a healthy, balanced diet. As a general rule as long as food is washed properly, cooked properly (especially eggs, meats and ready meals), and it is pasteurized, then you are pretty safe. Listen to your body – if it is craving certain foods, then usually there is something in that food that you or your baby needs (as long as it's not on the list of foods to avoid!).

DID YOU KNOW? Processed cheeses are OK, as are normal milkshakes and properly frozen ice-cream (just make sure it's pasteurized), as there is less risk of becoming infected with listeria. Peanuts are also fine too.

TOP TIP! If you are suffering from nausea, eating little and often can help. Often nausea is worse when blood sugars are low. So keep some ginger biscuits by your bed and nibble a few before getting out of bed in the morning. Keep some healthy snacks with you and keep hydrated. Sea-bands can help too. These can be purchased in most chemists. Try also to avoid wearing tight clothes.

DID YOU KNOW? *If your sickness is severe, you need to seek medical advice as you may be suffering from a condition called 'Hyperemesis Gravidarum'. This may need treatment with medication, or a hospital admission to help rehydrate you.*

 Try to quit smoking (and encourage your partner and close family to as well…. Much easier if you all do it together). You'll not only improve your health, but you'll be giving your baby a really good start in life, with less health problems later on…..it is the best gift you can ever give your baby. Whenever you decide to give up it will benefit you and your baby, so don't think 'There's no point quitting now as I only have a few weeks to go'.

…………. and babies are surprisingly expensive!

TOP TIP! *When you quit smoking, try and save the money you would have used buying cigarettes in a piggy bank, or savings account. See how quickly it mounts up….. And use it to treat yourselves or buy bits for your little one.*

So what does smoking do to your baby?

A cigarette has over 4500 chemicals in it. These include:

Anti-freeze ingredients.

Formaldehyde.

Carbon monoxide.

Hydrogen cyanide.

Tar.

Rat poison.

Ammonia (found in cleaning products).

When you breathe in, the smoke will go into your lungs, then bloodstream and eventually into your baby's blood stream via the placenta and cord.

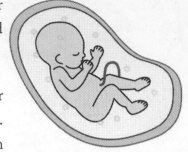

This will make your baby struggle for oxygen and its heart to work harder.... For up to 15 minutes after each cigarette.... Think of the cord as an oxygen pipe that you are relying on as a deep sea diver. A large sea monster then comes along and squeezes your oxygen pipe. You will then have to work harder to get the limited supply of oxygen, your heart will be under more strain as it works harder to pump the smaller amount of oxygen to where it's needed, and you will feel stressed. This is exactly what happens to your baby.

Smoking can increase the risk of your baby miscarrying, being born too early or at a low birth weight, or sadly being stillborn.

DID YOU KNOW? *If you quit and you are still around smokers, secondhand smoke exposure is harmful too.*

DID YOU KNOW? *As soon as you stop smoking, your body starts feeling the benefits within 20 minutes!!*

TOP TIP! *Avoid contact with lambing sheep due to the risk of Toxoplasmosis infection. Toxoplasmosis infection is also the reason to get someone else to clean out your cat's litter tray, and if this is not possible, wear gloves and wash your hands thoroughly afterwards. Also take care gardening and always wear gloves, as injuries can cause* *infections, especially if you have a cat, as they use the soil to go to the toilet in.*

<u>So you're set up now</u>:

You've told your partner who has probably exclaimed…….. 'REALLY?????..... I will need to do as much overtime as possible now'.

You may or may not have told close family and friends (lots of people wait until after their 12 week scan, but there's no right or wrong).

You've told the hospital where you want to have your baby (they still need to know if you want to have a homebirth too).

So, what next...........?

CHECKLIST

If you are planning a pregnancy then keep a note of the first day of your periods – it will be the first thing you will be asked when you tell a health professional about your pregnancy.

Book an appointment with your GP, or phone your local maternity unit for advice around about 6 weeks pregnant.

Buy those pregnancy multi-vitamins, and take as soon as possible (or before conception if you are planning a baby) – your baby especially needs folic acid and vitamin D.

Make yourself aware of foods to avoid in pregnancy.

Plan a healthy, balanced diet for both of you.

Sex is OK still as long as you haven't been advised against it, or are bleeding (in which case consult your GP).

Be very aware of your hand hygiene.

Avoid contact with lambing sheep due to the risk of Toxoplasmosis infection.

Toxoplasmosis infection is also the reason to get someone else to clean out your cat's litter tray, and if this is not possible, wear gloves and wash your hands thoroughly afterwards.

Take care gardening and always wear gloves, as injuries can cause infections, especially if you have a cat as they use the soil to go to the toilet in.

Stop drinking – the advice is absolutely no alcohol. What you drink, your baby has to cope with too.

Stop smoking – there is lots of help out there to get you smoke free. Pop a copy of your scan picture on your cigarette packet and think every time you smoke, your baby is deprived of the oxygen it needs.

Book your flu vaccine (between October–February).

Chapter Two

'Early days'

The next stage is your booking appointment. This usually happens before your twelve week scan, but does depend on when you have contacted the hospital, and how local pathways work. This is why it's good to tell your maternity unit in plenty of time so that an appointment and scan can be arranged.

Your Midwife will chat to you about your medical history and perform a risk assessment to decide on which maternity pathway best suits you and your baby.

 *TOP TIP! When you find out you are pregnant, ask your family (and get your partner to do the same if possible) about any conditions (with close relatives) that may affect your pregnancy.*

This includes:

Is there a family history of Diabetes?
Have there been any complications with pregnancies?
Are there any high blood pressure issues?
Have any babies been born with any problems?
Is there a family history of anxiety or depression?
Any medical conditions, such as heart problems etc?

Any information may be useful to your Midwife, so make a list.

TOP TIP! <u>Things to include on this list are</u>:

Have you had a smear test? If so when, and what were the results?

Find out if you have had Chickenpox as a child.

Do you work with children? – If so have you been screened for Parvovirus? (This will be discussed further on in the book).

What medications have you been on in the past (only long-term ones)?

What medications are you on now? (your Midwife will need to know their names, dosage and how many time a day they are taken)

It's easier to show your Midwife, rather than try and remember everything – as believe me; there will be a LOT of questions!

There are obviously occasions when knowing your family history is not possible. You or your partner may have been adopted, or maybe you aren't with the father of your baby. Don't feel bad. These things happen – your Midwife can still make sure you are safe without this information.

Set aside at least 90 minutes as this is probably one of the most important appointments. A thorough history is crucial to the rest of your pregnancy.

<u>If you have had other children, then the Midwife will need to know</u>:

The length of your pregnancy, along with the date of birth of your previous children.

Emma Cook

Some hospitals also may wish to know the time of birth.

Where your previous children were born.

Birth weights.

All easily (no it doesn't make you a bad parent!) forgotten.....

TOP TIP! *If you have had a child before, dig out those red books (child health records) and maybe any copies of your previous maternity records and bring them with you.*

As well as a thorough history, you may be asked to have a baseline set of observations and tests, including your height, weight, blood pressure and a urine test. You may also have to do a carbon monoxide test, which is a bit like a breathalyzer. This is done, regardless of your smoking status. It can sometimes pick up a faulty boiler in your house, or lactose intolerance, so it is important to take it if offered.

TOP TIP! *Try not to have a wee just before you see a Midwife!! Your Midwife will ALWAYS want a wee sample, so make sure you ask for a pot to do your sample in.*

The more you practice weeing in a pot in the early stages, then hopefully you'll become a pro by the time you have a bump adding to the difficulties of this necessary job!

Your Midwife will be able to tell a lot of important things from your sample, and this becomes more and more important as your pregnancy progresses. I will talk more about this in another chapter.

You may have bloods taken at this appointment (and your urine sent off to check for infection), but this depends on how many weeks pregnant you are, your hospital's policy and if you want early screening.

As I said earlier, this book is not meant to be a medical guide so I will not talk about screening for abnormalities in pregnancy. Your Midwife will discuss these with you on a one to one basis. They will also discuss all the blood tests available and make sure you are informed about every choice you make. There may be a consent form to sign. If you are not given a screening tests booklet, then make sure you are given the NHS screening website, which you can read through before your scan.

Although this is a really exciting time, your Midwife will have to discuss serious issues with you, and this is going to be the first major decision you make for your baby (One of many to come......)

Screening is not all about termination. It gives you choices. Imagine that you are told your baby has Downs Syndrome (as an example). Of course ending the pregnancy is an option, and you will be supported in this choice, but it could be that you could get more input from the medical team to ensure the best possible outcome for your baby.

The other benefits are 'fore-warned is fore-armed' – you can come to terms with the diagnosis and maybe meet other parents bringing up children with the same condition and join a support group.

Remember though that the initial screening does NOT diagnose a specific condition. The results only put you in a high risk or low risk group.

A high risk result is usually more than a 1:150 chance that your baby may have a problem (so that is 149 healthy babies for every 1 baby with a problem). If you had 149 chances out of 150 of winning The Lottery, who wouldn't buy a ticket?

So a high risk result doesn't mean your baby WILL have a problem, but you will be offered another test to confirm this.

A low risk result doesn't exclude a problem, but it is more unlikely.

DID YOU KNOW? *All scans are for a purpose – and that is to check on the well-being of your baby. Sometimes you may receive news that may not be as good as you had hoped (however this is not common), so it is always good to have someone with you when you have your scans – for the majority of women it's lovely to have someone to be part of a truly remarkable, happy occasion.*

At the end of this appointment you may be feeling a bit shell shocked. Lots of questions will have been asked and loads of information given to you.

You will have a set of maternity notes now (in my Mum's day it was a small postcard) – now it can be a set of many pages!!

 **TOP TIP!** *If you would prefer people not to know you are pregnant yet, take a big bag with you. The main giveaway of early pregnancy is carrying your notes around!*

TOP TIP! *Before you leave, make sure you know when your next appointment will be, and who it will be with. Ask your Midwife if you*

need to book it, or whether an appointment will be sent to you. When you get home write a reminder on your calendar (or for most people now input a reminder into your phone!)

Over the next week or so, slowly absorb the information within your notes.

TOP TIP! *Why not buy yourself a little notebook and write down things that you want to ask your Midwife about at your next appointment? Many pregnant women will tell you that their memory isn't the best!*

DID YOU KNOW? *Your notes need to become your best friend. <u>TAKE THEM EVERYWHERE</u>! Any appointment to do with your pregnancy, they need to come too. When you see:*

<u>*Your Midwife*</u>

<u>*Your hospital or scan*</u>

<u>*Your GP*</u>

TOP TIP! *Going on a long journey to see friends or family, or going on holiday? Take your notes too. They are a good source of information regarding your pregnancy and will help medical professionals look after you more easily when they haven't got a full history in your main hospital notes. Have them with you at all times if possible in your bag. If there is an emergency and you need to go to a hospital, far better to have your notes too.*

CHECKLIST

Check with close family if there is any relevant medical history and take a list with you.

If this isn't your first baby, refresh your memory on birth dates, times and weights (we will need full names, dates of birth and place of birth details for any children your partner may have too) to ensure the safety of your new baby.

Take someone with you if possible (especially to your scan).

Arrive in good time – especially if your booking is at the hospital. Parking can sometimes be an issue.

Take a drink and maybe a snack with you. Sometimes the room can be warm and in early pregnancy you may be feeling nauseous.

Avoid doing a wee just before the Midwife calls you in – if you need to go, ask for a pot at reception.

Take some money along with you for your scan photos (check with your hospital how much you need).

Find somewhere safe at home for your scan pictures, rather than leaving them in your notes. Check with the scan department before laminating scan photos, as the heat produced by laminating may damage them.

Take a good-sized bag with you to put your notes in if you don't want to advertise your pregnancy just yet.

Buy a little notebook and keep with your notes.

Make sure your Midwife has signed any relevant forms and you know what to do with them. The most common one is an 'FW8' form and is sent off to enable you to get a maternity exemption card. This entitles you to free prescriptions and NHS dental care whilst you are pregnant until your baby is a year old.

Other relevant forms may be given to you if you are on a lower income, or are under 18, to help you financially.

Make a note to remind yourself to book your next appointment (and where it will be).

Chapter Three

'Early appointments'

You will now hopefully be starting to feel better. Your hormone levels have settled and your placenta (the baby's life support system) is more mature, meaning hopefully one morning you wake up and all of the nausea has disappeared.

You may feel like exercising again, which is good for both you and your baby.

TOP TIP! *Best not to start any new exercise regimes, like running marathons, if you aren't used to it. If in doubt check with your health professional, and expect to slow down as your pregnancy progresses. Avoid things that are high risk, such as contact sports or those that will jar your joints too much.* <u>*Good exercises in pregnancy include*</u>*:*

Swimming
Walking
Static exercise bikes
Classes designed for pregnancy, such as aqua-natal and yoga

Your hospital may have sent you through a copy of your blood results and other paperwork relevant to your pregnancy, such as a growth chart and scan results.

As soon as you get these, place them safely in your notes so that you have them with you next time you see your Midwife.

TOP TIP! If you get sent your blood results, don't panic as a lot of values will be starred as 'abnormal'. Pregnancy values are different from the non-pregnant values the lab usually uses as a baseline.

Most hospitals send copies of your blood results to their antenatal clinic and your GP, so it is double checked. So no news is good news. If you are worried, then ring your Midwife or chat it through at your next appointment.

At your first antenatal appointment (usually around 16 weeks), your Midwife will explain your blood results and screening results to you.

If Group B Streptococcus has been picked up in your urine, or any infection, then now is the time to discuss this. You may have been sent a letter from your hospital informing you about Group B Streptococcus. This can be scary reading, but it is VERY common. Your Midwife will explain what your treatment is and what the implications are. Please try not to worry too much….. And don't read up about it on the internet!

Your Midwife will then discuss what needs to happen if you have a Rhesus negative blood group, and book you the relevant appointments.

<u>Relevant ONLY to those of you who have a Rhesus negative blood group:</u>

DID YOU KNOW? *If you are Rhesus negative (whatever your blood group is) – ANY bleeding from your vagina MUST be reported to your hospital, so they can advise you about what needs to happen. Don't ignore it as the hospital needs to know as soon as possible, so you can have an anti–D injection within seventy two hours of ANY bleed.*

Anti-D is an injection given to you if you are Rhesus negative, following any bleeding, and stops your body producing antibodies. Usually you will have an injection at 28 weeks, as a precaution. You will be advised to have this, even if you haven't experienced any bleeding.

A Rhesus negative red blood cell and Rhesus positive blood cell are seen as different to each other. If you are Rhesus positive you will have a protein on your red blood cell, called the RhD antigen. Lacking this protein means you are Rhesus negative. Rhesus negative blood is the rarer blood group (about 15% of the population), and so as we do not know the blood group of your baby, we have to assume it is the more common Rhesus positive one.

If any Rhesus positive bloods cells from your baby enter your bloodstream, then this can cause you to start making antibodies against the Rhesus positive cells (as they are seen as a 'threat')…. Think of it as a virus entering your body and your body producing antibodies to attack that virus to make you better.

If the injection, called 'Anti-D' to prevent antibody production is not given, then it can make your next pregnancy more difficult if you carry another Rhesus positive baby as your body will have made antibodies. This will then either cause a possible miscarriage or make your baby poorly and your pregnancy higher risk.

Welcome back to all Mums again!

Your Midwife may also discuss having a Whooping Cough vaccine at around 20 weeks. This is usually booked at your GP surgery, with the practice nurse. It is the same booster vaccine that is given to pre-school children and consists of Diphtheria, Polio, Whooping cough and Tetanus. It is offered to you during pregnancy to pass antibodies on to your baby. This then helps protect your baby in the first few months of life until they are old enough to have their own vaccinations.

As with any vaccination, this is a personal choice, but must be made with information provided to you, based on up to date research.

At every antenatal appointment, your Midwife will check your blood pressure and test your urine.

At your first antenatal appointment your Midwife may listen to your baby's heartbeat using a Doppler (this is a hand held device that is used by your midwife to hear your baby's heartbeat – you will be able to hear it too). An ear trumpet may be used first, called a Pinnards Stethoscope. Hearing your baby's heartbeat for the very first time is a really exciting time and so is great if your partner can come with you too.

TOP TIP! *Why not record your baby's heartbeat on your phone? A lovely way to treasure a special memory!*

DID YOU KNOW? *Sometimes your placenta can grow at the front of your uterus and this can make it more difficult to hear your baby in the early stages if they are hiding behind it. It also sometimes means that you don't feel your baby's movements as early as the placenta is acting as a cushion…. Your 20 week scan report will tell you where your placenta is.*

DID YOU KNOW? *Your blood system and your baby's blood system are separate? Your placenta carries oxygen and food to your baby, via the umbilical cord. Your baby then returns waste products to you to dispose of. So placental sounds on a Doppler are at the rate of your pulse. Fetal heartbeat and cord sounds are at the rate of the baby's heart – the cord sounding more 'whooshy' than the actual fetal heart.*

………….Ask your Midwife if you can hear all three sounds!

Your Midwife will then book (or get you to do it later) your next appointment and check that you have a date for your 20 week scan…. By which point you will have reached HALFWAY through your 40 week pregnancy!!

DID YOU KNOW? *Employers have to give you 2 hours paid leave to attend antenatal appointments.*

CHECKLIST

Remember to put any blood results and paperwork that is sent to you in your notes, for your Midwife to review.

Take your notes to every appointment.

If you are Rhesus negative, discuss what the plan is with your Midwife.

Remember to report ANY bleeding to the maternity unit if you are Rhesus negative.

Talk through the whooping cough and flu vaccines, so you can make an informed choice.

If you decide to have the whooping cough vaccine, remember to phone up your GP surgery and book it in with the practice nurse – your Midwife will tell you the best time to get this done. Sometimes your maternity unit may offer the flu vaccine in flu season. If not, this can be done at your GP's surgery too.

Take your phone with you to record your baby's heartbeat – and your partner, family member or a friend to share this special moment.

Remember to take a urine sample.

If you haven't had a date through for your 20 week scan appointment, get your Midwife to chase it up, or give the hospital a ring.

Avoid over research everything. Make a list of worries to discuss with your Midwife next time, or contact your Midwife or the hospital to stop and worries becoming out of control.

Chapter Four

'The pattern of care'

The rest of your pregnancy will follow a pattern as set by whether you:
Are low risk or high risk.
Have a BMI (Body Mass Index – a number worked out based on your height and weight) of less than or more than 35.
Are a heavy smoker.
Have a single or multiple pregnancy.
Are having your first baby or not.
Have any complications that arise during your pregnancy.
Have had a previous small baby (for the age they were born at).

 In this chapter I will tell you about what will happen at each ROUTINE antenatal appointment.........

Don't forget when you have an antenatal appointment to take:

Your notes
A wee sample
Any results etc. that may have been posted to you since your last appointment

Any forms you may need signing such as the Sure Start Maternity Grant, which is a one off grant given to people on lower incomes to help with the cost of a new baby. You are only able to claim for it once.

The general pattern for antenatal care for low risk Mums is:

8-10 weeks
Booking and bloods
Risk assessment
Carbon monoxide test
FW8 form and other relevant forms if on a low income, or under 18

11-14 weeks
Scan and screening bloods

16 weeks
Midwife appointment to discuss results
Discuss whooping cough vaccine

18-20 weeks
Routine scan

25 weeks
Midwife appointment (1st time Mums)
MatB1 form for working Mums
Book antenatal classes

28 weeks
Midwife appointment and bloods
Anti-D if Rhesus negative
Glucose tolerance test if indicated

31 weeks

Midwife appointment (1ˢᵗ time Mums)

28 week blood results

34 weeks

Midwife appointment

Blood test if on iron

36 weeks

Birth plan

Carbon monoxide test

38 weeks

Midwife appointment

40 weeks

Midwife appointment

41 weeks

Arrange induction of labour

If you have any risk factors, then your Midwife will have referred you to a consultant (a specialist Doctor in obstetrics – pregnancy and childbirth). They will then see you at the hospital and your care will be shared between the Hospital Doctors, Hospital midwives and your Community Midwife.

Usually you see a Registrar, who is a Specialist Doctor but works under the supervision of a Consultant. You may be seen by a Junior Doctor too, who will be overseen by the Registrar.

Each hospital appointment will be like any other antenatal appointment, but the Doctors and Specialist Midwives will decide on what extra things need to be arranged, such as scans, blood tests and extra appointments.

<u>At each appointment, your Midwife will</u>:

Check your urine (for protein and blood).

DID YOU KNOW? *As your pregnancy progresses, your Midwife will start to measure your bump to keep an eye on how your baby is growing. To get an accurate measurement your Midwife will need your bladder to be empty. So it's a good idea to have a wee JUST before your antenatal appointment – and as previously stated, as midwives are obsessed with your urine, you need to be able to provide a sample!!*

Check your <u>blood pressure</u>.

<u>Listen to your baby's heartbeat.</u>

TOP TIP! *As your baby gets bigger, your partner may be able to listen to your baby's heartbeat using an empty toilet roll. Place it where your Midwife found the heartbeat (however babies do move!), then get whoever*

 *is listening to put their ear on the open end of the tube and press gently down making a seal. They should then be able to hear the baby's heart. This is similar to a Midwife using a 'Pinnards stethoscope' – a sort of ear trumpet. This is often done before the Doppler is used.*

<u>Discuss anything relevant</u> to the number of weeks pregnant you are.

Emma Cook

<u>Take any necessary bloods or samples</u> to make sure you and your baby stay healthy.

<u>Give you time to ask questions, or discuss any worries</u>.

<u>At certain times throughout your pregnancy the following may be discussed</u>:

Carbon monoxide screening.

The whooping cough vaccine.

A **MatB1** is a form needed by employers during your pregnancy to arrange your maternity leave and calculate maternity pay. It cannot be given until you are 20 weeks pregnant, and so as you are not usually seen again until 25 weeks, this will be the time to get one. For most employers this gives them ample time to arrange your leave. However some like it as near to 20 weeks as possible. If this is the case, you need to contact your Community Midwife for an earlier appointment.

DID YOU KNOW? *You are entitled to 52 weeks of statutory maternity leave, and can start it 11 weeks before your due date.*

TOP TIP! *Check with your employer, job centre or citizen's advice bureau to see how much maternity pay you can claim, and whether you are entitled to any other help.*

TOP TIP! <u>*When leaving a text or message for your community Midwife, don't forget to put your FULL name at the end of the text..... They will remember you, but not always your mobile number!*</u>

Anti-D (for Rhesus negative Mums) – (See Chapter 3).

A **glucose tolerance test** will be offered to you at 28 weeks if:

You have a BMI of over 30.

Have a first degree relative (Mum, Dad, sibling) with diabetes.

Are of a high risk ethnic origin (your Midwife will assess and advise you if this is the case).

Have had a previous large baby (over 4.5kg).

Any other criteria that the hospital where you are due to have your baby have in their policy.

28 weeks bloods are offered to check that your baby is not using up too much of your iron, and to make sure you aren't making any antibodies in your blood.

 **How you are feeling?** Your mental health is really important too. Anything you say will be treated confidentially, and if you need extra support then your Midwife or Doctor will refer you to specialist services.

The **birth plan** and arranging the **option of induction of labour** will be discussed further on in the book.

CHECKLIST

Remember your notes for all appointments.

Remember your little notebook, with any questions or worries you may have.

Try and arrive at your appointment within good time, so you can rest beforehand. This means your blood pressure reading will be more accurate.

Remember a wee sample and as you get over 25 weeks, make sure you have a wee just before you see your Midwife so your bladder is empty and your baby's size can be measured more accurately.

Take any relevant paperwork with you.

Take any forms your Midwife may need to sign.

Make sure you know when and where your next appointment is.

Chapter Five

'Common pregnancy worries'

What common problems can happen in pregnancy and why?

If you want to blame anything for all those niggly complaints in pregnancy, then blame progesterone – that lovely hormone that is keeping your pregnancy healthy but having other less welcome effects on your body.

Progesterone makes smooth muscle more flexible, which is great for helping your baby into the world, but less great for day to day issues, such as:

Sore breasts are common in the early stages of pregnancy. Your breasts will begin to change in the first 12 weeks. Your body will start making tissue for producing and storing milk. They can become very tender, sometimes becoming larger and sometimes lumpy. White spots may be seen around your nipples. If in any doubt, get any symptoms, such as lumps, checked by your GP.

Morning sickness can occur during the day or at night and has been covered in chapter one, so not the best name to be given really!

Tiredness is very common as your body undergoes changes which reduce your energy levels. This usually disappears after about 16 weeks, until your bump gets bigger and heavier and the weight of your baby slows you down. On the plus side, you usually feel great from about 16-28 weeks!! If your tiredness is excessive, then talk to your Midwife as there may be underlying problems that will need checking.

Cramp happens as your muscles have to bear extra weight in pregnancy. They then feel the strain and your leg muscles may seize up in protest in the later stages of your pregnancy. It may even be painful enough to wake you from a deep sleep.

DID YOU KNOW? *Sometimes drinking a glass of milk and eating a banana before going to bed can help reduce cramps.*

Constantly wanting to have a wee is another delight of being pregnant. This happens due to increased hormones in pregnancy and later on is due to your baby pressing on your bladder. Again if it is worrying you, or if it is painful to wee, or you don't feel you are able to empty your bladder properly, this will need to be checked out.

Urinary infections can be more common as the progesterone hormone relaxes the smooth muscle of the tubes going from your kidneys to your bladder, which can lead to urine being trapped and thereby becoming infected.

TOP TIP! *Drinking diluted cranberry juice is a good natural way for preventing urine infections… but get advice before drinking it if you are diabetic or have been diagnosed with diabetes in pregnancy (gestational diabetes).*

Leaking of urine may be a problem as more pressure is put on the muscles of your pelvic floor (the layer of muscles that lie at the bottom of your pelvis and support your bladder). Sometimes a little bit of urine can leak when you cough, sneeze or laugh. To reduce the risk, try and do regular pelvic floor exercises throughout pregnancy.

SPD or Symphysis Pubis Dysfunction This can occur at any stage, and is due to the ligament holding your pelvis together becoming more relaxed. It can be very uncomfortable and the pain is felt at the centre, low down, where your pelvis is. You can sometimes have difficulty with walking and sleeping, and it can increase the risk of you feeling low in mood. Talk to your Midwife if it is worrying you as you could be referred for a physiotherapy assessment.

TOP TIP! *Try and avoid things that will stretch the ligament in the front of your pelvis. So try getting out of a car by keeping your legs together and swinging your body around, instead of putting one leg out and twisting your pelvis. This is important when getting out of bed too. You could also try sleeping with a pillow between your legs to keep your pelvis in a neutrally aligned position.*

Constipation happens as your bowel is made up of smooth muscle, and its' tone is not as good as it relaxes and becomes 'lazy' due to the effects of progesterone. Therefore food waste is not pushed through as quickly, sometimes leading to constipation. Also due to your pregnancy, your body will need to absorb more water from your food, making your stools harder and more difficult to pass. This can also increase your risk of getting piles (haemorrhoids).

TOP TIP! *Try and drink plenty of water (aim for about 2 litres a day) to keep hydrated during pregnancy. Also eat dried fruits, fresh fruit, vegetables and high fibre foods, such as cereals. This will all help at reducing the risk of constipation. See your GP if it is becoming a problem.*

Indigestion can happen as your stomach digests food slower and as your baby grows; your stomach becomes smaller to allow room for your baby. This can lead to the feeling of food wanting to escape and an acidy taste in your mouth. <u>Acid reflux</u> is common too as the opening to the top of your stomach has a flap (called the Cardiac Sphincter), which (yes you guessed it….. is made of smooth muscle). The action of the progesterone makes the flap flappier and therefore stomach acid can escape easily and make its way upwards towards your throat.

TOP TIP! *To help with indigestion, eat small, frequent meals. Sometimes drinking milk can help too. If you are struggling, contact your GP for a prescription to help reduce the acid in your tummy.*

Varicose veins are swollen veins found usually in your legs but can appear on your vulva too and happen due to the progesterone hormone making circulation slower.

DID YOU KNOW? *You can try and reduce the risk of varicose veins by*  *not standing for long periods. Sometimes compression stockings can help (ask your Midwife or GP as their size needs to be correct), and double pads in your underwear for vulval varicosities to apply some gentle pressure.*

TOP TIP! *Are you going away on holiday? If so, check with the airline as you may need a 'fit to fly' letter from your Doctor or Midwife. It's also a good idea to make sure they will allow*  *you to travel at your stage of pregnancy. Don't forget to wear flight socks, and keep hydrated and mobile on the flight.*

<u>Weight gain</u> varies from woman to woman, but a typical value is 10-12.5 kg.

<u>This consists of</u>:

The weight of your developing baby, placenta and amniotic fluid.
Growth of your uterus and breasts.
Increased blood volume.
Water retention.
Fat stores.

<u>**Ankles can become swollen**</u> due to the extra blood volume acquired naturally in pregnancy. This can also happen in your hands, feet and face. For more information on when swelling is more worrying, please refer to the next chapter (pre-eclampsia).

<u>Carpel tunnel syndrome</u> is caused by the nerve passing through a channel on the palm side of your wrist from your forearm to hand.  Sometimes this nerve can become compressed by the extra fluid you are carrying in pregnancy and causes pain, numbness and tingling in your fingers and thumbs. It usually disappears after birth, but sometimes you may need to be referred to a physiotherapist who can give you exercises, advice and maybe some hand splints.

TOP TIP! *If you are suffering from carpel tunnel syndrome, be very cautious when lifting heavy pans filled with hot water, or kettles, as your grip and sensation can be reduced.*

<u>Ligamental pain</u> is common as the baby grows, due to ligaments that stabilize your womb to your abdominal wall stretching as your baby grows.

<u>Back pain</u> is caused by softening ligaments that puts a strain on your lower back joints and pelvis. Help this by making sure you lift properly and support your back when sitting.

<u>Stretch marks</u> are usually related to your skin type rather than how much cream you put on – but don't deter from using cream as it may well help you feel you are doing something to prevent them – your baby will also love having a massage as you rub in the cream! Stretch marks start off as red lines usually on your tummy, hips and thighs and slowly change to a silvery colour after your baby has been born.

<u>Bleeding gums</u> are more likely due to pregnancy hormones. Any concerns, see your dentist.

TOP TIP! *Avoid having your teeth whitened in pregnancy until more research has been done.*

<u>Changes to your hair, skin and nails</u> are likely too.

Hormones make your hair grow faster (and therefore falls out more too) and become thicker. It can also react differently to hair dye.

TOP TIP! *Try and wait until after your 12 week scan before having your hair dyed, as the first 12 weeks are really important to your developing baby. The result of the final colour is a little more unpredictable in pregnancy too!*

TOP TIP! *Be careful with hair removal products as your skin may be more sensitive to them. Waxing and shaving are the best hair removal options.*

DID YOU KNOW? *If you need to treat yourself for head lice in pregnancy, a nit comb run through lightly conditioned hair, used thoroughly and efficiently, is now being suggested as the best means for anyone to get rid of nits. No chemicals are involved. If this method does not work, then I would suggest making an appointment to see your GP who can advise you further.*

Your skin will produce more oil too, so spots are more likely. However it can also have areas which are dry and itchy.

TOP TIP! *Calamine lotion or a non-perfumed gentle moisturizer is good at soothing itchy skin.*

Your nails become softer and can split and break more easily.

TOP TIP! *Try and keep your nails cut short to avoid them breaking and protect your hands by wearing gloves when doing the washing up or gardening etc.*

<u>**Chloasma**</u> is also called 'The mask of pregnancy' and is caused by your body over-producing melanin which leads to a browning of the skin. This can sometimes be seen on your face or tummy, and often worsens when you have been out in the sun.

<u>**Linear nigra**</u> is a dark line that can be seen in pregnancy running from your pubic bone, centrally up to your belly button. It's nothing to worry about and is usually seen in darker skinned women.

DID YOU KNOW? *Your skin is much more sensitive to the sun in pregnancy, so wear a high factor sun lotion when outside (apply it at least 15 minutes before going out).*

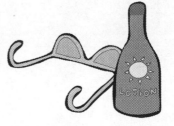

<u>**Thrush**</u> is caused by bacteria called 'Candida Albicans' and they unfortunately can thrive in your vagina in pregnancy because of higher levels of glycogen (a nice food source for them). You may notice a thick, white, itchy discharge. Ask your Midwife or GP for advice.

DID YOU KNOW? *Wearing cotton underwear, avoiding tight clothing and avoiding highly perfumed products to wash with can help. Eating natural yoghurt is a good tip too, but check it is pasteurized.*

TOP TIP! *Make sure you have a good dental hygiene routine and try to visit your dentist at least once in your pregnancy (you should receive free dental checks until your baby is a year old from an NHS dentist. Make*

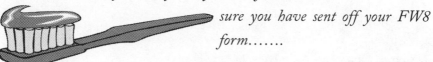

sure you have sent off your FW8 form.......

Lots of strange things happen to your body in pregnancy and you will have unusual feelings. If you are worried then talk to your Midwife. Most of the time you will be able to be reassured, and most of these common complaints disappear shortly after your baby is born.

CHECKLIST

Remember your body WILL feel different when you are pregnant. Most issues are common and normal. If in doubt, discuss your symptoms with your Midwife or Doctor.

Make sure as your pregnancy progresses you know which phone numbers to phone, and who to call for help when help is needed.

Allow your body to rest.

Avoid standing for long periods of time.

Listen to what your body is telling you.

Keep eating and drinking regularly.

Know where a toilet is at all times!

Ensure you are sitting and sleeping in a comfy position – invest in LOTS of pillows!

Eat a high fibre diet.

Make sure you are aware of how to get a physiotherapist referral if you need one.

Look after your teeth extra well and book a dental appointment

Look after your skin and don't forget sun cream.

Wear cotton underwear.

Try not to use highly perfumed products to wash with (especially when using it to wash intimate areas).

Chapter Six

'When should I talk to my Midwife?'

What are more worrying symptoms that you must not ignore?

Pre-eclampsia is a condition that can occur in pregnancy that you need to be aware of. This condition is the main reason you need to bring a urine sample to each antenatal appointment.

It can affect your liver and kidneys and there are some warning signs you need to look out for and tell your Midwife or the hospital immediately if you get any of them.

These include:

A severe headache (usually at the front or back of your head)
Visual disturbances, such as seeing flashing lights or 'floaters' in your vision
Swelling in mainly your face, fingers or feet
Pain under your ribs where your liver is – referred to as epigastric pain.
Sometimes raised blood pressure, but not always.

If you have ONE or more of these symptoms along with protein showing in your urine, then your Midwife will send you in to the hospital to be checked over – this usually means having some extra monitoring and bloods taken.

If Pre-eclampsia is diagnosed, then it can be monitored. You will need to be seen more regularly and a decision made to deliver your baby if your condition worsens.

If left undetected, pre-eclampsia can be harmful to you and your baby, so make sure you try and attend all of your antenatal appointments and take a urine sample. If you are unable to make your appointment, discuss this with your Midwife, as it will need to be re-booked as soon as possible.

Obstetric Cholestasis is completely different from itchy skin (usually felt on your tummy as the skin stretches as your baby grows) in pregnancy. Itchy skin is very common.....

HOWEVER:

Itching can also be a sign of something more serious, such as Obstetric Cholestasis, which affects how your liver works. If in doubt contact your Midwife. The difference is that:

The itching generally begins, or is most intense on your arms, legs, palms of your hands and soles of your feet.
The itching is usually worse at night.
It can cause you to have problems sleeping.
It can be linked to tiredness, poor appetite and nausea
It can make your skin or whites of your eyes to turn yellow (however this is rare).

This condition is due to bile (naturally occurring in your body, produced by your liver, and stored in your gall bladder, to help digest fats) leaking into your blood stream. It is the bile in your bloodstream that causes the extreme itching.

<u>It can be dangerous to your baby if left untreated, so seek advice as soon as possible if you think you may have Obstetric Cholestasis.</u>

The hospital will check your blood to see mainly how your liver is functioning. If these come back abnormal, showing you have this condition, then it can be well managed, with different drugs and delivery options. Your Doctor will discuss this with you.

Your liver will recover quickly after your baby is born, along with the itching, but that can take a few weeks to go.

<u>Parvovirus infection in pregnancy</u>

This is also referred to as 'Slapped Cheek Syndrome' or 'Fifth Disease'. As it is such a common infection in childhood, and sometimes only seen as a short-lived fever, most adults have immunity to it.

If you don't have immunity then you have a small chance of developing it in pregnancy if you are in contact with a child who has the illness.

DID YOU KNOW? *If you work with you children, or have a child who is due to start nursery when you are pregnant, it is worth having a chat with your Midwife about whether you need your blood testing at booking.*

You can then find out if you have immunity, and if you don't you are pre-warned to take extra care to avoid contact with children who may have the virus. If you come into contact then you must talk to your Midwife or the hospital as soon as possible as they will need to repeat your bloods about a month after contact. If you come back showing signs of infection, the hospital team will want to monitor your baby more closely with extra scans.

Chickenpox infection in pregnancy (also referred to as 'Varicella') if caught in pregnancy can cause problems too. Again, as with Parvovirus, if you have had it as a child (and you are more likely to know this than you will with Parvovirus), you and your baby will be protected by the antibodies in your blood.

If caught in pregnancy for the first time, it can make you and your unborn baby very poorly and so if you get any signs you may have Chickenpox, you will probably need to be given a live Varicella vaccine to help your body fight off the infection.

This vaccine needs to be given within 10 days of contact, and the earlier the better.

TOP TIP! If you are planning a pregnancy and you haven't had Chickenpox, speak to your GP, as they will be able to advise you as to whether to have your blood tested, and a vaccine if needed before you conceive.

Deep vein thrombosis can be more common when you are pregnant, and it is due to a blood clot developing in the deep vein in your leg. If this clots breaks off it can cause a serious condition called a 'Pulmonary Embolism'

If you get a pain in your leg or calf, and it suddenly becomes hot or swollen, seek urgent medical advice.

If you develop a sudden shortness of breath or chest pain, seek urgent medical advice.

<u>**Severe abdominal pain and bleeding**</u> can be a cause for concern, especially if at your 20 week scan you have been told you have a low lying placenta. Be sensible and seek advice quickly. If the bleeding is very heavy and you are not near a hospital, dial 999.

<u>**A variation in the pattern of your baby's movements**</u> can be worrying. Advice has gone away from 'Your baby should be kicking you at least 10 times a day', to 'Are the pattern of movements similar each day?'

Your baby will have his or her own little character as your pregnancy progresses, and as with any living being, will get into a routine. This is what we refer to as the 'pattern of fetal movements'. If your baby becomes very quiet or excessively busy, this can indicate that your baby isn't happy. Seek advice if the pattern you have been used to changes.

DID YOU KNOW? *Nowadays a lot of women buy a hand held fetal Doppler. It is fun to hear your baby's heartbeat, but please don't use it as a reassuring factor if you are worried. If it doesn't feel right, get your baby checked by a health professional.*

TOP TIP! *If your baby is quiet, try drinking a glass of ice cold water – that can often get him or her wriggling!*

TOP TIP! *Any worries call your hospital. They will probably ask you to come in and be monitored. After 26 weeks, you may be put on a monitor called a CTG. This prints out a trace of your baby's heartbeat. You wear 2 straps around your bump, which hold sensors. One sensor detects any activity in your womb, such as tightening's or contractions, the other monitors your baby's heart beat.*

DID YOU KNOW? *It is an old wives' tale that babies become quiet towards the end of pregnancy. The movements may feel different as your baby is more cramped, but the pattern of the movements should stay the same.*

CHECKLIST

Remember to attend all of your antenatal appointments.

Remember to do a urine sample for your Midwife or Doctor.

Talk to your Midwife, Doctor or hospital team if you have:

A headache that persists.

Experience problems with your vision.

Have pain where your liver is.

Have severe itching on your arms, legs, soles of feet or palms of hands.

Your skin or whites of your eyes are turning yellow.

Discuss extra blood testing with your Midwife if you work with young children.

Find out if you have had Chickenpox.

Remember – IF IT DOESN'T FEEL RIGHT, IT PROBABLY ISN'T.
Go with your instinct and call for advice if worried.

Chapter Seven

'Classes and Dad's'

By now you should have booked some antenatal classes, to attend when you are 30-32 weeks pregnant. This isn't compulsory (and they  aren't all about how to breathe! – I still get women saying to me 'When are we going to be taught how to breathe?), but for first time parents they are a good idea.

Not only do they give you loads of information, but it's a good way for you to meet other expectant parents and form friendships. Having a new baby can feel quite isolating, and so having someone to talk to or meet for a coffee is often much needed. No-one knows how you are feeling and what you are going through better than someone experiencing exactly the same thing. This is why internet forums have become so popular – however I'm old fashioned and think a face to face chat is more fun!

Dads can also have some 'Man time' – and discuss their worries. The baby's Dad mustn't be forgotten about. Pregnancy is mainly focused on you and they may be feeling anxious about a lot of things:

How life will change.

How they are going to cope with the extra responsibilities.

Financial worries.

What their role as a new Dad will be?

By chatting to other men going through the same thing, they will feel they are not alone.

The Dad's guide to birth goes something like this:

Don't faint.

Don't panic or break speed limits.

Wear something cool as maternity units are notoriously hot and labour can make you sweat.

Do whatever the Midwife and your partner tell you!

Do be patient and understanding if things get tough.

Massage her back and mop her brow – but ONLY when she says you can.

Never argue with a woman in labour.

Don't take anything said to you personally (she will have forgotten all about it when your baby is here).

Remain calm and relaxed – it will rub off on your partner.

Take lots of nibbles – labour can be long and can make you hungry.

Be in charge of the parking meter and post-birth phone calls (wait until your baby has been weighed as this is the first thing someone will ask!!)

It is also possible to pay for private classes as well if you prefer smaller groups, or maybe the hospital classes are fully booked.

If you are having twins etc. there are often specialist classes available, so ask your Midwife or phone your maternity unit for more information. There are also lots of local support groups out there for parents having a multiple birth, so get searching on the internet.

TOP TIP! Being in a larger group and asking a question can feel daunting, but I can promise you that someone is probably thinking exactly the same thing and will be eternally thankful that you have had the courage to ask!

TOP TIP! Take a cushion along as often the chairs are uncomfy!

One of the aims of your antenatal classes will be to empower you and think of labour in a positive way. When asked to describe what comes in to their heads when the word 'Labour' is spoken, the majority of people will say:

- Painful.
- Long.
- Stressful.
- Tiring.
- Scary.

Most negative thoughts are linked to fear of the unknown. If you understand the process, then you will believe in your ability, and hopefully you will think after antenatal classes is that labour is:

- Exciting.
- A journey to meet your baby.
- A means to an end.
- Exhilarating.

- Powerful.
- A happy occasion.

If you can come away from your antenatal classes thinking this, then your Midwife's job is done.

CHECKLIST

Remember to book your antenatal classes in good time, as they do get full quickly. A good point would be around the time of your 20 week scan.

Try and attend classes around 30–32 weeks of pregnancy.

Look into booking private classes if you prefer, which are usually smaller in size.

Classes are available for young parents and multiple pregnancies too.

Don't forget to invite your partner! Dads are important too. Try and involve him wherever possible.

Treat your partner to a book for new Dads – there are lots of good ones out there.

Take a cushion along to your class.

Maybe take a notebook and pen with you too.

Chapter Eight

'Preparing for your big day' and shopping for baby

You're nearly there now, around 6-8 weeks to go, so I am sure your thoughts have turned to LABOUR!... this may be more on your mind now after attending antenatal classes, where it all gets a little bit closer and a little bit more real!

Remember though that labour is a tiny part of the journey you will have with your baby. When you are pregnant, not many Mums-to-be can look beyond this day, which is very natural. So this chapter will talk you through how you make preparations for a more straightforward labour, which is a question often asked ....

Don't forget we are dealing with nature here. An unpredictable force. However one simple solution could be as easy as encouraging your baby to get into a good position for birth. This is often referred to as 'Optimal Fetal Positioning'.

 If your baby is head down then from 34 weeks onwards the advice is to get your baby to lie with its back on your left side

facing the front of you. This will help your baby engage (drop down into your pelvis) and make birth hopefully easier.

Think of your womb as a hammock. If you are sitting on soft sofas, and bucket shaped seats, your back will be curving in a 'C' shape…. Look at the letter 'C' and imagine that the letter is your spine. Your baby will want to lie nestled where it's comfy, and that will be following the shape of the curve of your spine with its spine. Therefore your baby's back will be lying against your spine and have its feet at the front of your tummy. This is called a 'Back to back position' written as 'OP' by health professionals, relating to the occiput (the back of the baby's skull) being posterior…..so your baby's face is looking at your tummy, not your spine.

As a baby needs to tuck its chin on to its chest to be born in a more 'stream-lined' shape, this is not possible with an 'OP' baby. The head circumference to deliver will be bigger, and this can lead to a longer labour and more chances of problems, such as needing help to deliver your baby.

Babies are more likely to get in this position in a modern western society as we are not doing as much manual work as women did 100 years ago, or out in fields hand harvesting crops anymore.

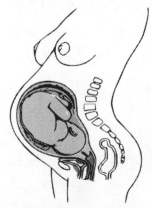

So you need you to get your baby looking backwards towards your spine with the back of its head facing the font of your tummy – an 'OA' position….. Occiput anterior, as shown in the drawing below.

Your baby can be helped into this position by avoiding your spine becoming 'C' shaped.

Good ways to do this are:

Sitting on a Birthing Ball

DID YOU KNOW? Your Ball needs to be pumped up enough so that when you are sat on it; your knees are lower than your hips. If the Ball is too soft, then it will be like sitting in a bucket seat again and therefore will not help.

Regularly try and sit more upright and adopt forward leaning postures. Your tummy will then become a hammock for your baby instead of your spine, encouraging your baby into a good position.

If you are sat on a squashy sofa, try putting pillows under your bottom and in the small of your back. This is a good idea when driving too.

Turn a kitchen chair around and sit on it leaning on the back of the chair, so that your legs straddle the chair and your arms rest on the back. Again make sure your knees are lower than your hips. (This position may be too uncomfortable if you have a sore pelvis – referred to as Symphysis Pubis Dysfunction 'SPD'), referred to in Chapter 5.

Sit to read at a table, with your elbows on the table and knees apart, leaning forwards.

Kneel on the floor and lean over a bean bag to watch TV.

Get onto all fours and wash the kitchen floor.

Go swimming on your front.

When you go to bed lie on your left side, with a pillow between your legs and your top knee resting on the mattress.

TOP TIP! *Try doing some of these exercises/positions when you are having Braxton Hicks. These are painless tightening's that can happen in later pregnancy. Your tummy will have the feeling of hardening, without being painful. It can help your baby get in a good position even more.*

Avoid:

Sitting with your legs crossed.

Using squatting as an exercise in late pregnancy as your baby's head may be forced down into the pelvis before the baby has manoeuvered into a good position.

 The next question that is often asked at this stage is 'When do you think I will go into labour?' So as not to get too despondent, let me explain something that people often don't think about, and it will hopefully make more sense.

At the beginning of your pregnancy, your Midwife will ask you for the 'date of the first day of your last period'. This is because this is where your pregnancy officially starts from. However, you usually ovulate (release an egg to be fertilized)  about two weeks later. Therefore, for two weeks, you actually aren't pregnant. Your baby is two weeks behind where you think.

This is why it is safe to let a low risk pregnancy go to 42 weeks, as your baby has then grown for 40 weeks. After this your placenta may be getting a bit tired, which is why many hospitals will be thinking about inducing you, something your Midwife or Doctor will discuss with you. If there are any risk factors present, your Doctor may want you to be induced earlier, but they will discuss this with you and allow you to make a choice after you have been given all the information.

TOP TIP! *Think of your due date from any time between 37–42 weeks – a 'five week' due period. Only a tiny number of babies are actually born on their due date!*

A baby is classed as 'term' instead of 'pre-term' at 37 weeks. They are usually able to sustain themselves without much help then. So if your baby is born at 37 weeks, then remember, they are not '3 weeks pre-term', which will hopefully put your mind at rest.

At around 36 weeks, your Midwife should be discussing a 'Birth Plan' with you.

TOP TIP! *Try not to be too rigid with your birth plan. If you are and the labour you hoped for doesn't happen, this can lead to feeling as though you are a failure – which you definitely are not. Who else has kept your baby alive? – You and your amazing body.*

Have a little think about what you would like if possible, but keep your options open. Make some notes which will help you and your Midwife when you are discussing this.

Ideas for your birth plan include:

Where would I like to have my baby?

What do I need to pack in my bag?

Who will be with me at the birth?

TOP TIP! *Choose a maximum of 2 people to be with you. They need to fill you with strength and make you feel safe. These birth companions need to be consistent to enable you to progress well in labour.*

TOP TIP! *Avoid having a van full of people waiting in the entrance to take it in turns to support you! Often a new person entering the room can have an effect on labour and slow it down for a short time.*

Do I know the number to ring when I am in labour, or if my waters break?

Do I know how to get into the maternity unit if the front doors are locked?

Does my birthing partner know where to park?

How will my baby's heartbeat be monitored?

How can I stay active during my labour?

What positions are best for labour?

What pain relief options do I have?

When may I need to have an episiotomy?

How do I want my placenta to be delivered?

Am I happy for my new baby to be given vitamin K, and if yes, how would I like it given?

Do I want my baby to be delivered straight on to my skin after birth?

Does my birthing partner want to cut the baby's cord?

How do I want to discover the sex of my baby?

How am I going to feed my baby?

Am I aware of how to reduce the risk to my baby of 'Sudden Unexplained Infant Death Syndrome'?

Is there anything that is worrying me that I need to discuss with my Midwife?

All of the above are pointers, and will be discussed in the next few chapters in more detail.

 Start to buy things for your baby nice and early to avoid last minute panic – unless you want to get yourself into labour! Included below are some things that are essential, and some things that are handy. Newborn babies don't need thousands of pounds spent on them. They need love a feeling of security, food and to be kept clean. Save your money for when they are teenagers and they get REALLY expensive.

Newborn baby essentials:

Either a pram / buggy / travel system – chat to other Mums that you know, or to the staff in the shop. Think about your lifestyle needs.
Car seat (if not buying a travel system).
Moses basket, mattress and stand.
Cotton, hand knitted or cellular blankets (NOT fleece).
Cotton sheets.

Long sleeved sleepsuits.

Short sleeved sleepsuits / vests.

A few cotton or hand knitted cardigans.

A few hats.

Scratch mits.

DID YOU KNOW? *A good way to stop scratch mits falling off your baby's hands is to sew a few thin pieces of ribbon to one side of the mit. They can then be tied on and won't fall off.*

Snowsuit depending on the season.

Changing mat.

Nappies.

Nappy bags.

2 different coloured small pots.

Cotton wool.

If breast-feeding – a nursing bra and breast pads.

If bottle feeding – milk, bottles, bottle brushes and a sterilizer.

TOP TIP! *Even if you are breast-feeding, it's handy to stock up with a bottle of sterlising fluid. Useful for nipples shields and breast pump parts. You don't need to rush out and buy these, wait and see if your Midwife advises buying them.*

Bibs and muslin squares.

Kitchen roll.

Washing up bowl.

Some monochrome toys.

Soft nail file.

Baby shampoo.

TOP TIP! *Either peel the long bits off of your baby's nails as they are quite soft to begin with, or file them down gently with a soft nail file. Try not to nibble them as this may cause an infection. Cutting them with clippers can be a challenge when baby is wriggling!*

<u>Handy to have but not needed immediately:</u>

Changing bag with changing travel mat.
Changing table (the top of a chest of drawers is equally ideal).
Baby towels.
Breast pump.
Sun shades for car windows.
Pram shade.
A sling.
Bouncy chair.
Play mat.
Baby monitor.
Bath thermometer.
Nappy wrapper.
Bottle preparation machine.
Grow bags to sleep in when baby is over 10 lbs in weight.

In the next chapter, I will discuss what you need to pack in your maternity bags and useful things to buy for you for after the birth.

TOP TIP! *When you go on maternity leave and are getting to the 'bored stage', why not cook batches of easily frozen, nutritious food that you can then live on for the first month or so? Easier than cooking and healthier (and cheaper) than surviving on ready meals and takeaways:*

Emma Cook

<u>*Ideas include:*</u>

Casserole and stew

Lasagne

Macaroni cheese

Pasta bake

Cottage pie

Fish pie

Curry

Homemade pizza

Soup

...... and loads more I am sure (cookery isn't my forte!)

CHECKLIST

Avoid sitting on squashy, soft chairs, sofas or bucket shaped seats (if you have to, prop yourself up with pillows. Invest in a birthing ball and make sure when it's pumped up, your knees are lower than your hips when you're sat on it.

Birthing balls come in different sizes (based on your height), so check you're buying the right one.

Sit on a kitchen chair back to front when possible.

If you are reading, try sitting at a kitchen table with your elbows on the table and knees apart.

Kneel on the floor and lean over a beanbag or floor cushion to watch TV.

Swim on your front.

Lie on your left hand side in bed.

Support your hips by placing a pillow between your knees when resting.

Avoid sitting cross-legged.

Don't forget your baby is two weeks behind what you think you are.

Your due date can be any when between 37-42 weeks.

Think about discussing your birth plan with your Midwife around 36 weeks.

Keep your birth plan flexible.

Make notes of things you would like to discuss with your Midwife before your birth plan appointment.

Have 1-2 people with you during labour that you feel confident and relaxed with.

Make a shopping list, and get batch cooking.

Chapter Nine

'I want my pregnancy to be over now!'

When you are about 36 weeks pregnant, you should be thinking about packing your hospital bag.

There are lots of different lists available, but from a practical point of view, I would suggest the following:

A SMALL LABOUR BAG:

TOP TIP! _As tempting as it is to take a big bag with you, try and keep it as minimal as possible. Firstly a large bag can take up too much room and can be an issue if there is an emergency. Secondly if your Midwife needs to find something quickly, it is far easier in a smaller bag._

Your maternity notes.

2 large packs of maternity pads.
Disposable or cheap underwear that can be thrown away.
A t-shirt for labour.
If you are planning a water birth, a bikini.

Boiled sweets and energy drinks.

A goodie bag for your birthing partner(s).

A hairband if you have long hair.

Music for labour.

A flannel.

Dressing gown.

Slippers.

Clean nightwear.

Wash stuff.

Dark coloured bath towel.

DID YOU KNOW? *You don't need to worry about bringing baby towels, sheets or blankets as most maternity units supply these when you are in hospital.*

A few nappies.

An outfit for your baby, including a vest, babygro, hat, scratch mits, socks and a cardigan.

DID YOU KNOW? *Even if it is boiling hot, babies can take about 24 hours to regulate their temperature, so need to be kept nice and warm. Think of getting out of a warm bath on a really hot day – you will feel cold. This is how your new baby will feel at first.*

Camera.

Phone.

Phone charger.

Change.

A large bag for dirty clothes to go in.

Ready to use baby milk (starter packs with sterilized bottles and teats can be purchased from most large retailers) if you wish to bottle feed.

TOP TIP! *Check with your Midwife as most maternity units now only supply ready to use baby milk if it is medically indicated.*

A SLIGHTLY BIGGER POSTNATAL BAG

Your baby's red book (you should have been given one from your Health Visitor).
Some more packs of maternity pads.
Extra clothes for you and baby.
A pack of nappies.
Muslins and/or bibs.
Top (face) and tail (bum) pots (2 small different coloured plastic pots) for washing your baby with.
Cotton wool.

TOP TIP! *Cotton wool and warm water is far gentler for baby's delicate skin.*

A bag for dirty washing.
Nursing bras.
Breast pads.
Box of tissues.
A pen.
A book or magazine.
Some treats for you to nibble on.
More baby milk if bottle feeding.

TOP TIP! *This postnatal bag can be kept in the car, along with the baby's car seat. If you need to stay in, then your labour bag can be taken home and your postnatal bag will be fresh, clean and organized! If you don't have to stay in, you can just unpack when you are home.*

TOP TIP! *Make sure you are aware of how to fit your baby's car seat into your car safely and that it fits properly.*

DID YOU KNOW? *A lot of retailers will offer a service to check it fits properly when you have brought your car seat.*

<u>*I always think it may be a good idea to tell well-meaning family members and friends that your due date is 2 weeks later than it is!! This would reduce the risk of a million texts as soon as your real due date arrives…..*</u>

Any news?

Have you had the baby yet?

Blimey this baby doesn't want to make an appearance eh?

How much longer?

All of these lead to you feeling utterly useless, which leads to stress, which in turn reduces the lovely hormones that you need to actually go into labour, so a vicious cycle starts.

As long as your baby is happy and growing normally, there is no need to hurry the natural process of labour.

<u>A few reasons not to push for an earlier induction:</u>

If nature is forced, then she can be more unpredictable.

If your body isn't ready to have your baby, then induction will be a more difficult process.
Once intervention starts, it can carry on in your labour.

TOP TIP! *Embrace your pregnancy. Your body is the best home for your baby until he or she is ready to come.*

Enjoy those last few weeks and meet up with friends, do some things for you – life with a new baby is completely different. You have waited a long time for the day you meet your baby, but if your baby decides to stay put, then a few weeks is not a huge amount of time (Imagine you are having a Valentine's dinner and look ahead until Christmas Day – a long time. Now fast forward to the middle of December. That is how far you have come – and Christmas Day is just around the corner!)

There are many natural ways to try and encourage your baby to make an appearance, and these are safe from 37 weeks (when your baby is officially 'term' and therefore ready to be born).

DID YOU KNOW? *You should always check with your Midwife or Doctor before using ANY method to get labour started, especially if you have:*

Complications during your pregnancy
Complications with your blood pressure
Diabetes, Kidney or thyroid problems
A multiple pregnancy or breech baby
Had a previous rapid delivery
A planned caesarean booked
Had a caesarean before

Had a previous premature baby
Had any bleeding after 12 weeks

!!IF IN ANY DOUBT, CHECK BEFORE USING!!

Some things to try are:

Aromatherapy oils that relax you are a good start. Labour is based on your body feeling comfortable and ready to have your baby. If you are stressed and worrying about when you will go into labour, then it is less likely to happen naturally. Good relaxation oils include:

Tangerine.
Mandarin.
Grapefruit.
Bergamot.
Ylang ylang.
Lavender.
Frankincense.

Mix 2 drops with a base oil for massage, or add a few drops to your bath.

TOP TIP! *A good way to think of why relaxation is so beneficial is by using the analogy of a gazelle grazing in the African plains. If they are in early labour, and a lion suddenly appears, the gazelle will be flooded with adrenaline (the fight or flight hormone), and her labour will stop to allow her to escape the lion. So take this time to relax in any way that works for you. Your baby will love this too.*

<u>**Clary sage**</u> is an essential oil, and can make your contractions start.

<u>Ways to use are:</u>

A few drops can be added to a bath enable you to inhale the aroma (about 4 drops is sufficient).

A few drops can be mixed with oil (grapeseed or almond) and massaged into your skin (a hand, tummy and feet massage is a lovely way to relax).

Make a compress with a flannel. Soak it in a small jug of warm water, with a few drops of clary sage added. Lay the flannel on your back, neck or tummy.

A few drops can be burned in an aromatherapy candle burner.

Maybe put a few drops on your pillow at night.

It is actually used in many homebirths and birthing units if contractions have slowed, and can be very effective. Other aromatherapy oils have different functions and are useful in labour too. Your Midwife can discuss this with you.

***DID YOU KNOW?** If you have friends, family or visitors that are in the earlier stages of pregnancy, they should not be around this oil. It can be dangerous in earlier pregnancy because of the effects that it can have.*

<u>**Raspberry leaf tea**</u> can help tone your womb muscles so that they can hopefully be more effective when you go into labour. Try and start drinking it from 32 weeks. Start with one cup a day, and slowly build

up to 3 cups a day. If you start having strong tightening's (Braxton Hicks) after drinking a cup, then listen to your body and cut down on the amount you are drinking. Raspberry leaf tea is completely different to raspberry fruit tea (which won't do any good!), so check what you are buying to avoid wasting money.

DID YOU KNOW? *'Braxton Hicks pains' are usually painless tightening's that happen towards the end of pregnancy. This is your body's way of training for the work ahead. Getting the muscles in tone to deliver your baby successfully. They are completely different to the contractions you will have when labour starts.*

Eating spicy foods may help but may just give you indigestion! If you fancy a night off of cooking, it may be a good ploy!

Eating pineapples is in theory good, as it has a chemical in the fruit that can help soften your cervix, but it is in such low amounts, you'd have to eat about 7 pineapples to see any effect!

SEX! – Joking aside this method can be very effective as the sperm has a small amount of prostaglandins in which are used to induce labour.

In summary:

Relax.
Don't be too fixated on the due date that has been given to you.
Enjoy the last few weeks by doing nice things for you.
Spend quality time as a couple.
Think of it in a positive way – each day is a day closer.

Stock up on the things listed below to help after your birth:

Paracetamol.

Ibuprofen (don't take when you are pregnant).

Tea tree oil.

Lavender oil.

Arnica tablets.

Haemorrhoid cream.

Non-scented soap and shower products.

Chocolate!!!

All those things you couldn't eat in pregnancy and were craving!

CHECKLIST

Pack your bags for hospital by 36 weeks.

If your health visitor hasn't been in contact, give your surgery a ring and see if you can pick up a red book (Child Health Record).

Always buy purpose designed maternity pads, rather than super-plus pads, or those pads with 'wings'.

Buy some large pants, or disposable pants that are a size bigger than you would normally buy.

Enjoy the end of your pregnancy, rather than wishing it was all over.

Meet up with friends.

Enjoy time with your partner.

Avoid wanting an induction of labour if there is not a medical reason to need one.

Start drinking raspberry leaf tea from 32 weeks.

Try other methods to start labour from 37 weeks.

Remember to check with your Midwife or Doctor it is safe to do this beforehand.

Look in to hiring or buying a TENS machine (see Chapter 10).

Stock up on those postnatal essentials.

Chapter Ten

'I'm in labour!'

The big day has FINALLY arrived. You've waited a long time, and now you are shortly going to meet your baby.

In this chapter I am going to talk about the early phase of your labour, and good ways to cope.

You may have had a few false starts, which is entirely normal for those of you having a first baby.

When you are pregnant, and not in labour, your cervix (which is the entrance to your womb), is a fairly long, closed tube. In the centre of your cervix will be a plug of mucous, which when it comes away is referred to as a 'show'. This plug has protected your baby by making it very difficult for any bacteria to enter your womb.

DID YOU KNOW? *The hospital doesn't need to know about a show. It's an exciting thing to see as it means things are starting to happen. As long as it is a mucous plug, and not offensive in smell, or fresh blood, then start getting excited. Your baby is on his or her way.....*

When you are nearly ready to have your baby, your cervix will start to shorten and eventually become completely flat. This process is called 'effacement' and happens for up to a week or so before you go into labour. As your hormone levels are highest at night time (I will explain why this is more when breast-feeding is discussed), and as your cervix thins out, you may feel niggles of pain (effacement pains), and may see your show coming away, as your cervix becomes shorter.

As soon as it becomes day, your hormone levels drop, and so your pain can subside. This can be exciting and then disappointing, but please know that this is totally normal and a process that has to be gone through.

For those of you who have had a baby before, your cervix can often be 2-3cm open at the end of your pregnancy and so you can go into labour without the effacement stage needing to be done. The positive thing about this is that the process is quicker, but often without as much warning.

TOP TIP! *Make sure your birthing partner has their phone with them at all times and has made plans for what to do when you phone. This may be made easier by discussing options with their boss, and being located more locally if travelling is a part of their job.*

I once reassured a lady who was having her first baby that even though her husband worked 2 hours away, there would be plenty of warning. She had a 50 minute labour and her husband missed the whole thing. This is VERY rare, but can happen, so make a plan! (They both forgave me! – however I have always been very careful what I say to families ever since that day).

So what is best? Stay at home or rush straight to the hospital?

Staying at home is by far the best option for a Mum with no risk factors (if you need to go in as early as possible in your labour, the team looking after you will have advised you of this)

TOP TIP! *If you can stay at home for as long as possible in labour, then you will often make better progress.*

TOP TIP! *Make sure you have transport arranged. A friend or family member on stand-by if your birthing partner doesn't drive. Make arrangements for your other children to be cared for – and don't forget about your pets too!*

<u>**Only dial 999 in an emergency**</u>. Getting you to hospital in labour if everything is progressing normally is NOT an emergency.

Your home is your castle. It's the place you feel safe, and the place where you will be more relaxed. As discussed in the previous chapter, if you are relaxed, then the good labour hormones will be free to do their job. Labour doesn't like adrenaline (one of the stress hormones), and if you go in to hospital too early, the adrenaline may slow or even stop your labour.

Labour will start off feeling like period pains do, and then the pain will gradually build up in intensity and contraction length. It is often described as a 'wave' of pain starting from the top of your bump and washing over your tummy. Eventually, your contractions will be strong and regular, usually happening every 4-5 minutes, and lasting for up to 60 seconds.

DID YOU KNOW? *There are three stages of labour:*

FIRST STAGE *- from the time your contractions are strong, regular and painful until you start pushing your baby out.*
SECOND STAGE *– when your cervix is fully opened until you push your baby out.*
THIRD STAGE *– delivery of your placenta.*

The first stage of labour will be discussed in chapter 11, and the second and third stages in chapter 12.

TOP TIP! *Any abdominal pain before 37 weeks, or that is constant (without a break) needs investigation, so make sure you know which number to phone.*

DID YOU KNOW? *Any fresh bleeding needs checking out too. Fresh blood is not normal.*

Your waters may or may not break – either is fine. Your baby is safely enclosed in a double bag of membranes, which keeps the baby's environment clean. Think of your baby's head as a cork. When the head is down low ready for labour and your waters break behind the baby's head (the hind waters), you may only feel the odd trickle of fluid.

If your fore waters break (in front of the baby's head), there is nothing to block the fluid coming out, so a large gush is felt.

If your waters break, the hospital needs to know. A large gush is an obvious sign, but sometimes the trickle of water is hard to notice, and may be confused with urine leaking. Your waters will have a very distinctive smell, and will not smell like urine does. People often describe it as a 'bleachy smell'.

The first things the hospital will ask you are:

1. What time did your waters break?
2. What colour is the fluid?

DID YOU KNOW? *Waters and black underwear aren't a fab mix! So if you think your waters may have broken, pop a maternity pad on. You will then be able to see the colour and assess how much is coming out by the weight of the pad.*

TOP TIP! *Don't ignore a trickle – best to get it checked. If your hind waters have broken, then any tear in the membranes can let infection get in, which is why hospitals have policies on when labour needs to be helped if your contractions haven't started.*

What can you do to stay at home for as long as possible?

Don't stick too rigidly with going in to hospital when your contractions happen once every 5 minutes, especially with a first baby.
Go in to hospital when YOU feel the time is right… You'll know when.
If you are coping, stay at home.
Have a warm bath.
Distract yourself by watching a film, sleeping or going for a walk.
Take regular paracetamol at intervals as stated on the packet.

Use a TENS (named as it uses 'Transcutaneous Electrical Nerve Stimulation' to block the pain messages to your brain, and to stimulate your body's natural painkillers - endorphins) machine.

DID YOU KNOW? A TENS machine can be either brought, or hired from well-known stores. Make sure it is a maternity TENS machine and NOT a physio TENS machine as the frequencies are different. Do not use a TENS machine before 37 weeks, and read all the instructions before use.

TOP TIP! If you are using a TENS machine and want to have a bath, obviously electric gadgets and water don't mix. Once it is taken off it seems to work well if put on again within 30 minutes. After this time my experience is that you have to start back at the beginning again and slowly build the pain relief up from the start.

Ring the hospital for advice, if unsure. They will be able to assess what the best plan of action will be.

Think of labour as a positive experience.... Your body is designed to do this.

Emma Cook

CHECKLIST

Expect some 'false starts', especially when you are having your first baby.

Don't worry about your 'show' – it's a good sign things are beginning.

Fresh bleeding is NOT normal, so ring the hospital.

Make sure your birthing partner's phone is charged, on and with them at all times.

In early labour, try and stay at home for as long as possible.

Keep calm and relaxed.

Go into hospital when YOU feel the time is right.

Remember the midwives at the hospital are there to help and advise you, so don't ever feel frightened or alone.

<u>*When you go into hospital, don't forget your:*</u>
Hospital notes.
Red book.
Labour bag.
Postnatal bag.
Car seat.
Phones and money.

Have a plan for your other children, and don't forget about your furry friends too.

Chapter Eleven

'I CAN do this'

The time is probably now right for you to venture into the maternity unit (or maybe call your Midwife to come to you if you are having a homebirth).

To all Dad's out there, or would be F1 drivers, drive carefully. It isn't like in the films, where a woman has one contraction and the baby pops out. I wish it was, but reality is that even when labour is established....... Strong, regular contractions that efficiently widen the exit for the baby...... it can be 12-14 hours for Mums having their first baby, and 6-8 hours for Mums who have had a baby before. This is even before the task of pushing has begun.

TOP TIP! *To all birthing partners out there, don't use your drive to hospital to practice for Monaco. Remember the rules of the road have to be adhered to, especially red lights!*

Mum's to be need to wear a seat belt to stay safe on the journey to hospital.

TOP TIP: *When pregnant the safest way to wear a safety belt is for the lap strap to sit over your hips, comfortably under your bump. The diagonal strap should fit between your breasts, and around your bump. Basically the belt nestling around, not over your bump.*

TOP TIP: *If your waters haven't broken yet, pop an old shower curtain or waterproof pad on the seat. It saves a lot of stress!*

Unfortunately, as well as speed limits and road rules needing to be adhered to, this applies to parking too. I always think traffic wardens love maternity units. People have other things on their minds and often forget a ticket – so they will leave you a little surprise on your return if you aren't careful.

Usually outside the front of most maternity units, are designated drop-off zones or 20 minute bays. These can be used if needed. It gives enough time to get settled and then move the car when things are calmer. Often wheelchairs are near the entrance if needed too.

TOP TIP: *If the wheelchair is acting as though it has had too many gins, then it is often easier to pull it, rather than push. Often hospital ones are slightly different!*

Make sure you find out how to actually get into the maternity unit. These days, for the safety of the patients, the doors are often locked. There will be an entry camera or buzzer, but make sure you are aware of where it is and how it works. Ask your Midwife, or do a trial run.

When you arrive at the maternity unit, or your Midwife arrives at your home, a history will be taken and your Midwife will go through and discuss your birth plan with you. Midwives LOVE paperwork – a necessary thing, but always remember that you will come first. It may appear that all your Midwife is doing is writing a novel, but she (or he) will be constantly keeping a watch over you. Notes will be taken and often a graph filled out, called a partogram. This is a picture of your labour, your progress and how your body and baby are coping.

TOP TIP: *Before your Midwife leaves the room, make sure you have been shown where the call bell is and how to use it. Sometimes labour wards can be like ghost towns as everyone is in a room looking after other women in labour, and it can be hard to find someone.*

DID YOU KNOW? *More males are training to become midwives now, and they do exactly the same job as their female counterparts. You wouldn't think twice about a male Doctor so a male Midwife is no different. However, they will understand if for religious or personal reasons, you would prefer not to be looked after by a male Midwife.*

Your initial check will include …..

Yes, you guessed it a URINE SAMPLE!!
Your blood pressure.
Your temperature.
A feel of which position your baby is lying in.

A listen to your baby's heartbeat with a Doppler (the machine you have been used to seeing at your antenatal appointments).

DID YOU KNOW? *In labour your baby's head can get a bit squished when you have a contraction, and sometimes their heartrate drops a little. This is quite normal during a contraction and as babies are masters at coping with lower oxygen levels to us, they cope well.*

A tired or stressed baby will tell your Midwife by continuing to drop their heartrate after your contraction has finished. So for this reason, your Midwife will listen in at the end of your contraction, for approximately a minute to assess how well your baby is coping.

If your baby is showing signs of distress, then more monitoring will need to be started. The most common way is by popping you on a machine called a CTG. This was discussed earlier in Chapter 6. Your baby's heartbeat and your contraction readings will be traced out on a bit of graph paper, and shows how your baby is coping. It's a bit like a heart trace when you have an ECG at your Doctor.

DID YOU KNOW? *A baby's heart rate isn't designed to go along at the same rate, like ours does at rest. The sign of a happy baby is a heart rate that varies, and is anywhere between 110 – 160 beats per minute.*

If it is proving difficult to monitor your baby's heart beat with the tummy strap, it may be necessary to pop a little clip on your baby's head to monitor it safely. You will probably notice a little scratch on your baby's scalp, which will heal very quickly.

Remember, labour is NOT a test of endurance, but a means to the safe arrival of your baby. You are in good hands, and if it is too painful and you can't cope, then in developed countries, we are lucky enough to have lots of options available:

KEEP ACTIVE, MOBILE AND RELAXED.

TOP TIP! *Think of you pelvis as a flexible opening. If you are lying down, then the exit route for your baby will be narrower as your pelvis won't be able to open as much to allow baby to be born.*

So good positions for labour include:

Stay on your feet as much as possible.

When you get a contraction, lean forwards and rock your hips from side to side. Wiggle your bum!

Hang on to something so you can let your body go floppy at the same time as turning your knees outwards.

Use you birthing partner as a piece of 'equipment' to lean on. This can be with them sitting on the edge of the bed, and you supporting yourself with your arms on their shoulders. Or they could be sat in a chair and you could kneel down on the floor with your knees apart, as you lean on their thighs.

If you want to be on the bed, get on all fours instead of lying down. If you do need to lie down, then lie on your side, preferably your left side.

In the first stage of labour, your baby needs to do a few twists and turns to negotiate your pelvis and enter the world. Nature is extremely clever and your ligaments soften allowing your pelvis to become more flexible. If your baby is in a good position then keeping upright and mobile will lead to, on the whole, a less painful and faster labour. Bones in your baby's soft skull are flexible too to allow your baby's head to change shape, making birth easier for everyone.

TOP TIP! *Think of walking a tightrope across a very high canyon. If you stay calm, relaxed and focused on the where you are heading, you will achieve the crossing. If you stop midway, look down and panic, then you are going to be in trouble.*

ALTERNATIVE WAYS TO RELAX

Some women explore other methods of pain relief, and these include acupuncture, reflexology, or vocalization – in simple terms making a load of noise to cope with the pain. Aromatherapy will be discussed later.

HYPNOBIRTHING

Special courses are available but this method needs a lot of preparation when you are pregnant. You will need to use a CD during labour that your body has become accustomed to relaxing to. Sometimes there are key words that shouldn't be used, such as 'pain' or 'painful'. Hypnobirthing is all about positivity. Put your wishes in your birth plan and discuss with your Midwife on arrival.

BIRTHING POOL

A lovely way to relax. Imagine you have severe tummy pain and you get in a warm bath – what happens? Well the pain becomes more manageable as your body relaxes with weightlessness and warmth.

A birthing pool is a larger version of a bath and comes in various shapes, sizes and designs, often with well-placed handles and steps or seats to sit on. Some that you can hire for a homebirth even have drink holders, so you could even imagine you were on the beach on holiday!

DID YOU KNOW? *Some women find taking a rubber ring in with them to use in the pool is a help and something to hang on to! – Just remember not to bite it!*

AROMATHERAPY

Great used alongside relaxation techniques and the birthing pool. Your Midwife will be able to advise you on what aromatherapy oil is needed at which point in your labour.

If you are having your baby in a higher risk unit, it may not be possible to use certain oils as there may be women in there that this may be dangerous for.

GAS AND AIR

This is also called nitrous oxide, Entonox or laughing gas. It is a mixture of nitrogen oxide and oxygen.

TOP TIP! *Try not to wait for your contraction to be painful before you start to breathe the gas and air. Start breathing it as soon as you feel a NIGGLE that your contraction is starting.*

Your pain relief will be much better, because a contraction is usually 50-60 seconds long, the peak being around 25-30 seconds in. If you start breathing the gas and air in only when your contraction is painful, this will mean that as the contraction fades off the gas and air will be working at its best. Get it into your body early and it will mask the peak, which is the part that you may find difficult to cope with. Stopping the pain at that point will mean you will cope a lot better.

TOP TIP! *A contraction is either building up to, or coming down from the peak. Think of climbing a mountain. Not all of the contraction will be unbearable.*

DID YOU KNOW? *You can stop breathing in the gas and air as your contraction starts fading? This means that you won't be as high as a kite!! You will still be getting pain relief for about 20 seconds after you stop breathing it.*

PETHIDINE

This is a drug, similar to Morphine that is given by an injection into a muscle. It has the effect of not so much as stopping the pain, but making you have the feeling that you don't care about the pain.

DID YOU KNOW? *Pethidine is great for early labour if it is dragging on. It can let you settle down and sleep for a few hours, and often you will wake up and then labour efficiently as you have got some energy back.*

Pethidine is not great for the later stages of labour, and is best not to be given a short time before your baby is born. This is because it crosses the placenta in small quantities and can make your baby sleepy (like it does to you). This can make establishing breast-feeding more difficult.

REMIFENTANIL

This is a fairly new type of pain relief to maternity, but has been used in general medicine following operations. This may not be available everywhere yet, but is an alternative to an epidural. It is a very short-acting strong pain killer. It is referred to as 'Patient Controlled Analgesia' as it is administered by a machine that will give a small dose when you press a button. Like having a drip, you will need a tube inserted into your hand, or arm before the drug can be given. The pump will be safely set up by a specially trained Doctor, so that you are unable to give yourself too much of the drug.

EPIDURAL

Maybe this is what you thought would need as soon as you got into hospital, but I hope after reading this book, then your opinion may have changed.

Epidurals do have their place, and if you need one then don't feel a failure, as you are not. Every labour is different, and every person has their own way of coping and pain threshold.

If you can try and cope using the techniques I have discussed, then give it your best shot, and use the epidural as your last resort.

DID YOU KNOW? *An epidural has to be given to you by a trained Doctor, called an Anaesthetist. Usually there is only one Anaesthetist on labour ward, so if they are in theatre dealing with an emergency, or with another woman, there may be a little wait.*

<u>Even if the Doctor is there as soon as you decide you want an epidural, it is not a quick fix method:</u>

The procedure needs to be explained.

You need to sign a consent form and understand the risks.

A needle will have to be popped into your hand and a drip started so that if your blood pressure drops then it can be fixed.

Then the Anaesthetist needs to arrange all of the things that they will need in a sterile way.

The Anaesthetist then has to clean your back and make the area sterile (this is COLD, COLD, COLD!!)

The next step is giving you a local Anaesthetic to numb the nerves in your skin.

Then the Anaesthetist inserts a needle into your back. Attached is a sterile syringe either filled with sterile water or air. The needle is slowly inserted until it reaches a space in your back called the epidural space. The Anaesthetist will feel a drop in pressure when the syringe is gently pushed, and they will then know they are in the right place.

 **TOP TIP!** *To help the Anaesthetist, arch your back like a cat stretching. Push your spine out towards where the Doctor is standing behind you. This will open up the bones in your back and make it easier to insert the needle.*

DID YOU KNOW? *When the Anaesthetist says that they are in the epidural space it is VITALLY important you stay as still as a statue.*

Once the needle is in the epidural space, then a sterile clear plastic tube with a coloured tip will be thread into the needle, so it sits in your spine, and the needle will be removed. At this point you can relax a little.

The plastic tube has a coloured tip so that your Midwife can check that all of the tube has been removed after labour.

I once heard a woman discussing with her friend behind me in a queue about how she had had a needle left in her back for the whole of her labour when she had an epidural.

I promise you this would never happen – the needle is out and disposed of as soon as possible.

The tubing will then have a padded cover popped over it at the point it exits your back, and the rest will be taped up your back, and will dangle over your shoulder with a filter.

From the filter another tube will be attached to a syringe which is attached to a machine that delivers a set number of mls of the drug over a set period. This can be adjusted to manage your pain, and extra drugs can be given directly through the filter if you need an extra dose.

Before the pump is set up, a test dose will be given by the Doctor to make sure the epidural tube is in the right place and is working.

So the reasons why I say think carefully before opting for an epidural are that you are lying in bed and this is the position that makes delivery harder for the reasons I have discussed earlier. I have only ever seen one epidural work where the woman was totally pain free and was able to kneel on the bed and move around well.

It can increase the need for an instrumental delivery of your baby or a caesarean, both of which will be discussed in the next chapter.

DID YOU KNOW? *A mobile epidural will not let you jump out of bed and walk around pain free (if I am wrong, then I apologise to my Anaesthetic colleagues!). The name simply means that you can sort of move your legs in bed.*

I had every pain relief option in labour, except reminfentanil as it wasn't available when my son was born. I even had an epidural for 20 minutes!! – This was obviously for research purposes for this book!

<u>If your labour slows down, there are a few options:</u>

Sometimes all your body needs is a bit of energy. A spoonful of honey can sometimes get contractions going again.

It may be as easy as getting up and moving around to help gravity push baby's head onto your cervix, encouraging contractions to start again.

If your waters haven't broken, that may be an option. The Midwife will use a little instrument that looks like a crotchet hook. It will be sterile and single use.

DID YOU KNOW? *When the Midwife is trying to break your waters, they will have to wait for you to have a contraction.*

The best way I can explain why is thinking about a balloon with only a small amount air in it. It changes shape and moves away when you apply pressure. When you get a contraction, it is like squeezing the half empty balloon, so all the airs gets pushed into a smaller area. The balloon then becomes tight and will be easier to pop.

If all of the above fails and your waters have broken, then the Midwife may discuss starting you on an artificial hormone drip to kick start your contractions, or make them stronger and more effective.

DID YOU KNOW? *The artificial hormone drip will only work if your waters have broken.*

This is why induction of labour can be a lengthy process. The hormones that are used initially are purely to get your cervix open enough for your waters to be artificially broken, so the hormone drip can be started to manage labour. Induction can take 24-48 hours before labour even starts, so if you need to be induced (maybe your baby is refusing to come out) – go in with the mindset that it will be a LONG process, then you won't be too frustrated.

So relax, and stay calm and positive. Don't feel you are a failure if things don't go as you hoped or planned. The main thing is that you and baby stay safe.

This is your motto for labour. Be positive. YOU CAN DO THIS. Each contraction is one nearer to finally meeting your baby.

TOP TIP! *The womb is a muscle and needs energy to carry on contracting well. You wouldn't run a marathon with no calorie intake, so why would you do the same in labour? If you are unable to eat for medical reasons, then a drip is normally put up to do this job.*

CHECKLIST

Before you set off for the hospital, don't forget your notes, hospital bag and baby's car seat.

Stick to speed limits on your way to hospital.

Invest in a cheap shower curtain and sit on it in the car if your waters haven't broken yet.

Stay as upright and as mobile as possible during your labour.

If you are using gas and air, start breathing it as soon as you get the first twinge and stop breathing it as the contraction lessens.

If able to, then continue to eat and drink during your labour to give you energy.

If things don't go as planned, then still be proud of what you have achieved

Chapter Twelve

'Nearly there'

When you get to the point of not being able to stop yourself pushing, then you will have reached the second stage of labour.

You're nearly there!!!!

You will have gone through a short 'transition stage' where most women think they:

"Can't do it ....."

"Want a caesarean......"

"Want to go home......"

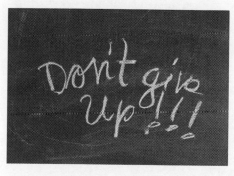

When the transition stage is over, your cervix will have finally reached the magic 10cm, and you may find the second stage of labour more bearable than the first stage. You know the end is in sight, and can at last do something positive with each contraction.

Out of nowhere usually comes a spurt of energy. Nature's way of helping.

Your contractions may slow down or even stop for a short while when you reach this stage. It's like your body is regaining strength for what is truly 'The last push'.

Before you start to push, then your Midwife will encourage you to do a wee. Your bladder sits in front of where your baby's head is now. A full bladder can make it more difficult for baby to get out, and may become bruised by baby's head pressing into it. When you start pushing it will feel a bit alien to begin with, and it can take 5-10 minutes to get into the swing of it and feel what to do. Your Midwife will be there to explain everything to you and give you lots of encouragement.

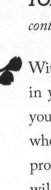

TOP TIP! *Only push when you are having a contraction, or you will wear yourself out.*

With each contraction, the muscle fibres in your womb shorten and so slowly help your baby out. If you have an epidural, then when you reach 10cm, your Midwife will probably advise resting for an hour. This will make it easier for you to push your baby out as nature will have helped baby travel down with each contraction over the hour.

There are lots of theories on the best way to push. Some say chin on chest, hold your breath and push like you are having a poo. Others go with making noise to help. The main thing that will help is being upright so your pelvis can open out and allow baby more room.

TOP TIP! *If you want to deliver your baby by squatting, unless you are an Olympic skier, then do exercises during your pregnancy to strengthen up your leg muscles. A good exercise is leaning with your back against a wall, and squatting down, increasing the duration over a period of time.*

You will feel pressure down below, and you may even do a poo. There is nothing to be embarrassed about. As your baby's head gets lower, your bowel gets squashed, so anything that is in the way will be pushed out. Midwives are experts at subtly getting rid of things like this, and if your bowel is empty, then that allows more room for baby to come.

DID YOU KNOW? *You are no longer subjected to a routine enema and shave!*

Each push, as with each contraction, is one step nearer to cuddling your baby. **As with the first stage, stay positive and focused. You will feel like you are going one step forwards and two steps back. This is normal!**

If you are having your first baby, all the muscles around the baby's exit route have never done this before, so they need to be stretched slowly. It will feel like you have been pushing forever and nothing can be seen. This doesn't mean that nothing is happening – it will be.

You will then get to the point where the Midwife will say 'I can see a bit of the head now'. Keep going...... the little bit of the head will feel like it's going back up the way it came, but with each push, a little more of the head will be seen.

Some women like to watch their baby's head coming out with a mirror. If this isn't your cup of tea, then no worries, but it can be a good way to encourage you. Most maternity units will have access to a mirror, so ask if one is available.

Once your baby's head has stretched your muscles sufficiently, it will quickly get to the point of crowning – usually for a first time Mum, about an hour after pushing has started. Your Midwife will then inform you to 'PANT'..... And it's just that. Little tiny blows of air out of your mouth. This will stop you pushing your baby's head out too quickly. Yes this bit will sting a lot, but your baby's head will be delivered with the next contraction. Concentrate on your Midwife at this point. Often Dad's get very excited when they see baby is nearly here, and a battle can ensue between Dad shouting 'PUSH' and your Midwife shouting 'DON'T PUSH, PANT!!'

Babies don't appreciate being born quickly. They much prefer a slow delivery which allows the pressure in the baby's head to adjust as it is born. Also your vagina won't appreciate the baby's head speeding out. All of the muscles down below cope much better and a less likely to tear badly if they have been allowed to stretch slowly.

If baby is getting tired and is telling the Midwife by a dropping heartbeat, the Midwife may decide at this point to do a little cut called an 'Episiotomy'. This will deliver baby more quickly.

A cut may also be done if the Midwife thinks you are going to tear badly. What the Midwife will try and avoid is a tear going down into your bottom, as this can be trickier to heal.

Usually a local Anaesthetic will be given before the cut is made.

With the next contraction, your baby's head will be born.

Your Midwife will then check around your baby's neck for a cord. It is fairly common for babies to have their cord around their neck. If the cord is loose enough, the Midwife will either deliver your baby's shoulders through the cord and untangle baby as he or she is born, or simply slip the cord over the baby's head.

DID YOU KNOW? *Babies need to wiggle their shoulders around inside of you when their head is born, so there is a little break to allow baby to do this.*

If your baby has come out as planned, the first thing your baby will see is your bottom! As the shoulders come through your pelvis, then the baby's head will turn to look left or right, depending on which position baby is in.

Once baby's head has turned, then usually another contraction happens fairly quickly. Your Midwife may help guide your baby's shoulders under the front of your pelvis, by gently pushing baby's head towards your bottom. Once one shoulder is free, the baby follows quickly.

DID YOU KNOW? *If you are having a water birth, the water is kept at body temperature so your baby is not at risk of drowning. It has come from an environment of fluid. The important thing is not to bring your bottom up out of the water when baby's head has been born. As soon as fresh air hits baby's head, he or she may start trying to breathe.*

This is the moment you have been waiting for. Your little bundle is  FINALLY safely in your arms.

As much as this is a joyous moment, don't feel bad or guilty if you are not overcome with emotions of motherly love. You may well be worn out and just want to catch your breath. This does NOT make you a bad mother. Sometimes that flood of love can take days or weeks to happen…. and it is different with each Mum.

One thing your Midwife may have discussed with you is what you want to happen when your baby is delivered. Some people prefer baby to be dried with a towel before being placed on them. Most people just want to see their baby, so as baby is delivered, then your Midwife will hand you your baby immediately. Either way is fine. The important thing is that your baby gets skin to skin contact as soon as possible, for as long as possible.

Benefits of skin to skin contact for you and baby are huge……..

It regulates your baby's temperature.
It reduces stress levels.
It reduces pain.
It promotes bonding.
It makes breast-feeding easier.
It improves your baby's immunity.
It reduces postnatal depression.

TOP TIP! *Do as MUCH skin to skin contact as is possible for as long as you can. Skin to skin contact doesn't have to stop when you baby grows out of the newborn stage.*

DID YOU KNOW? *Dads can do skin to skin contact too – even in the delivery room, if you don't feel up to it. It's a great way to help them bond with baby too.*

When you look through your notes after the birth, you may see a section referred to as the 'APGAR score'. This is a score which is given to your baby out of 10, usually one minute and five minutes after birth. The closer the score is to ten, the happier your baby. A score under seven may mean baby needs a little bit of help to get going.

Don't be scared if your baby doesn't breathe or cry immediately – they are still attached to their cord, which will still be providing them with oxygen. A lot of things happen inside your baby's body in the first few minutes of life. With the first breath, air enters the lungs (which didn't happen when baby was in your womb) and fluid is forced out into the baby's blood stream, filling the lungs with air and inflating them. A newborn baby looks very purple, and as the first few breaths are taken, the colour will become pinker. This is completely normal, and your Midwife will be keeping a close eye and assessing whether your baby needs any help. There may be two midwives in the room at this point, one to keep an eye on baby and one to keep an eye on you. This will depend on your hospital's policy and way of working.

When your Midwife is happy with baby, the next decision to make is for the third stage of labour. Far less exciting, but still a vital stage – the delivery of your placenta.

There are two choices:

Let nature take its' course.
Let drugs help speed the process up.

DID YOU KNOW? *Some hospitals give you the choice to donate the blood in your placenta for stem cell research? Ask your Midwife in the antenatal period about this....Or you could get the stem cells harvested and stored (at a cost) for future use if your child becomes sick.*

If you opt for a natural delivery of your placenta (and there is no real need to have any drugs if everything up to this point has gone normally), then your baby's cord will be left attached until your Midwife is unable to feel a 'pulse' in it anymore. This is usually approximately 15 minutes after birth. This allows the small amount of blood that is in the placenta to be returned to your baby. The cord will be clamped and cut when the pulsing has stopped and then slowly your placenta will separate from your womb, the cord will lengthen, and with a few pushes, your placenta will be delivered after 20-40 minutes.

 TOP TIP! *Do you or your birthing partner want to cut the cord? Have a chat about this towards the end of your pregnancy.*

TOP TIP! *If you are Rhesus negative, your Midwife will take a small amount of blood from one of the vessels in the cord shortly after birth (this won't be painful for you or baby). The blood in the cord is baby's blood, so it can be sent off to the lab to see what blood group your baby is, and if Rhesus positive, you will need anti-D, like you had in pregnancy. This saves having to physically take blood from your baby.*

If your placenta refuses to budge, then when other things have been tried, like making sure your bladder is empty, getting you into different positions and breast-feeding your baby, another option may be to have it manually removed in theatre by a Doctor. This is done with good pain relief, and you will be given an antibiotic course afterwards to reduce and risk of infection.

When your placenta is safely out, your Midwife will check it carefully to make sure nothing is missing, the condition it is in, and that there are two membranes and three vessels in the cord. If you want to see what was feeding your baby and helping him or her grow, ask your Midwife if she can show you. It really is fascinating.

DID YOU KNOW? *Your placenta is your property, so you can take it home if you wish.*

- *Some people want the placenta left attached to their baby, and it is covered in a variety of herbs, lavender seeds and salts etc and carried around in a specially made bag. (This is called a lotus birth).*
- *Some people make placenta print pictures which resembles a tree.*
- *Sometimes you may want your placenta to be made into a smoothie, or capsules.*

However often the most popular choice is usually throwing it in the bin!

Then when you thought everything was FINALLY over, the one last check your Midwife will have to do is check whether you need any stitches. This won't just be a case of a quick look on the outside, as sometimes tears can happen internally. Take this chance to have a last go on the gas and air. It is better if the Midwife has a thorough look and nothing is missed.

If you do need stitches, then this will be done under local Anaesthetic, with dissolvable suture material, in sterile conditions.

 Then you can have the best cup of tea and slice of toast in the world!

YOU DID IT!!!!!!!!!!!

CHECKLIST

Only start pushing when you cannot control your body wanting to push.

It is normal to feel you aren't getting anywhere to begin with.

Listen to your Midwife when they ask you to pant.

The slower the birth of your baby's head, the better for both you and baby.

If you are having a water birth, then make sure you keep your baby's head under the water until their body has been born.

Do as much skin to skin as possible after birth – if you don't feel up to it then let Dad or your birthing partner do it.

It is normal for your baby to look a bit purple straight after birth and not breathe immediately.

If you wish to breast-feed, then try and get baby to breast-feed as soon as possible.

Chapter Thirteen

When your baby has other plans

Maybe your baby has a different plan and doesn't fancy coming out as he or she should do. If this is the case, then there are options to make sure your baby (and you) stays safe.

We are very lucky to have high tech maternity units now, but normally birth is a completely natural process. If your baby has other ideas, then so be it. The aim, as I said earlier is the safe delivery of your baby.

So, what are your options?

VENTOUSE DELIVERY

Babies, like Mums, get tired in labour. They often tell the Midwife they aren't happy with the pattern of their heartbeat. If baby is in a good position and has been trying really hard to be born, but both of you have run out of energy, then the first option to think of to help you would be this one.

A ventouse is a flexible soft cup that attaches to your baby's head with the help of suction, and as you push, the Doctor can help guide your baby out. People often think it resembles a sink plunger!

DID YOU KNOW? *You still have to push when you're having a ventouse delivery, but the ventouse will help with the end bit.*

When a baby is born following a ventouse, they often have quite a 'cone' shaped head, with a round bruised area where the cup has been placed. Don't panic – babies are experts at healing themselves, and the head will recover within a few days.

Sometimes the Doctor may need to help your baby out with a small cut, but this isn't always the case.

FORCEPS DELIVERY

Forceps are often referred to as 'BLADES'. This can sound a bit scary when you hear the Doctor asking for a blade, but they are designed to cradle baby's head and like with the ventouse, help guide baby out.

Forceps deliveries are normally needed when baby has got itself in an awkward position, or is too high up to come out easily with a ventouse. Again the Doctor helps baby come out when you have a contraction, and if you are able to push, the Doctor will ask you to push if needed.

Usually forceps deliveries are performed in theatre, and you will be given very good pain relief. This is because there is always a risk that the forceps delivery may not be possible, and it will have to proceed to a caesarean.

Forceps are also sometimes used to assist premature deliveries, by protecting the baby's head from the force of birth.

Imagine a set of salad servers – this is what they look like!!

You baby may be born with a few forceps marks on their face, but as with the bruising on the baby's head following a ventouse, these will heal very quickly. Better to have a few bruises, than to have a distressed baby.

CAESAREAN SECTION

A caesarean is only performed if absolutely necessary. They come in three degrees of urgency:

1. An elective or planned caesarean.
2. An emergency caesarean.
3. A crash caesarean.

Elective caesareans are often performed for known complications, such as a breech baby (bum first), or if you have had a caesarean following your first baby and opt to have another one. You will be given a planned date and time, usually when you are 39 weeks pregnant. By this time your baby's lungs have matured enough to cope with a planned caesarean. Before this, there can be some breathing issues as baby hasn't been stressed during labour.

Even if you are given a date, it may be cancelled at the last minute. Doing an elective caesarean is dependent on theatres and Doctors being free. If there are lots of emergencies happening, then obviously they will take priority and you may be asked to go home and come back at a later date.

TOP TIP! *Think of an A+E department. You are sitting in the waiting room and there are only a few people in there, but the waiting time is 6* *hours. You will be thinking that this is ridiculous, but you cannot see all of the very poorly people coming in by ambulance in another entrance. On the surface things appear calm, but it will be manic behind the scenes. No-one wants to cancel an operation, or keep you waiting, but as the Doctors and midwives are dealing with nature, then each hour is unpredictable. They will be prioritising care – and would do the same if your baby or you were struggling.*

If you or your baby were struggling, then an emergency caesarean may need to be done, and this would be prioritised by a Doctor.

Most caesareans will be done under either a spinal Anaesthetic (an injection of a drug into your back), or an epidural. Your Anaesthetist will determine which the best option is and discuss the options with you. If at all possible a general Anaesthetic (when you are put to sleep) are avoided. If the caesarean is for a life-threatening situation, then putting you to sleep will be the fastest option.

Your birthing partner will be able to come into theatre with you (after he or she has got changed into theatre scrubs) when the Anaesthetic Doctor is happy. This will only be if you are having a spinal or epidural and are awake during the operation. If a general Anaesthetic is needed, then your birthing partner will wait in a room for news as everything has to be done very quickly.

In theatre, there will be lots of people:

An Anaesthetist.
An Anaesthetic Assistant.
A Midwife.
A Scrub Nurse/ Midwife.
A Runner.

A Surgeon.
A Surgical Assistant.
Possibly a Student.
Possibly a Paediatrician (Baby Doctor).

That's a minimum 7 people, which is completely normal. Many people think that something awful must be happening to them as there are so many people in the room. Everyone needs everyone else for the team to work, so please don't worry.

DID YOU KNOW? A lot of maternity hospitals will teach medical and Midwifery students. The students have to log a certain number of witness births, deliver a set number of babies and gain experience with lots of other skills. They are our future – the ones who will be looking after your baby when he or she has a family.

TOP TIP! Students are always supervised (they have to be, as they are practicing under their mentor's registration). When they are coming up to qualifying, they may be working more on their own, but there will be someone supervising them and constantly checking them. It is your choice entirely whether you are happy to have a student help to look after you.

When your birthing partner enters the theatre, things will happen very fast. By this point you will be pain free, have a drip up, have had a little shave, have a catheter in to drain the wee from your bladder (this will stay in until the day after your operation), have had an antiseptic wash on your bump, and have sterile gowns covering all of you except your bump and face!!

The Anaesthetist will test your spinal or epidural before the Surgeon starts operating. This is either done with some tweezers to see if you can feel anything, or with a cold spray. They will be assessing you constantly.

DID YOU KNOW? *Women often describe having a caesarean as 'Having the washing up done in their tummy'. You will still be able to feel pulling and prodding, as your baby is born, but with obviously no pain. This often worries women, but is normal.*

Just before the Surgeon starts, a screen will be put up in front of you (made up of sterile drapes, so please don't touch it). If you would like to see your baby being born, then you can ask for the screen to be dropped at the point your baby is coming out. Sometimes the Surgeon will need to use forceps if baby's head is low. If everything is OK, then skin to skin contact is still the best option.

You will hear loads of weird noises in theatre – as it would be for an operation when normally you are fast asleep. These include the beeps of the monitors, sounds of suction to help suck up the fluid that baby has been in, clattering of instruments. Try and zone out and listen to some music instead. 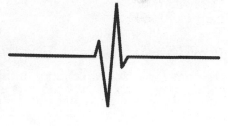 Your Anaesthetist will be there chatting to you to try and take your mind off everything. Focus on the fact you are going to meet your baby very soon.

Sometimes a machine called a 'DIATHERMY' is used to help stop bleeding by heating the skin and small blood vessels to seal them off. This can sometimes smell a bit odd, like smoke, but again is perfectly normal.

The point from the Surgeon starting to your baby being born is usually only a matter of minutes!!

Your placenta will then be delivered and come out the same way as your baby has done. The Surgeon will then check for any bleeding, and start the process of stitching up your cut.

DID YOU KNOW? *The cut will be made low down on your tummy, so that when your hair grows back, the scar will be hidden – this is why it is often referred to as a bikini line cut.*

As the stitching is coming to an end, Dad will probably take baby into recovery, whilst the final parts of your caesarean are being performed. You will follow shortly afterwards, after a dressing has been applied to your wound (like a big plaster), and you have been cleaned up and moved onto a clean bed.

Sometimes baby will be weighed and checked in theatre, exactly as would happen after a vaginal delivery. However it may all be done in recovery. This entirely depends on how the hospital you have your baby in functions.

If you have had a general Anaesthetic, if possible, the Midwife will wait until you have woken up, so that you don't miss out on watching your baby be weighed and checked.

TOP TIP! *Don't forget a caesarean is major abdominal surgery. Women forget that as they have a baby, but you still need to be careful. If you have a toddler, sit or kneel down to hug them, rather than trying to lift them up as you normally would.*

DID YOU KNOW? *Most insurance companies will not let you drive a car for 6 weeks after your operation, and I'm afraid you won't be able to hoover (I know – I can tell you're devastated), or lift anything.*

You will have to be in hospital for at least 24 hours, and as soon as the Midwife is able to, they will get you out of bed to sit in a chair for 5-10 minutes. Your drip will come down as soon as you are able to tolerate eating and drinking.

TOP TIP! *When you are in bed, try and keep your ankles and feet moving regularly to keep the blood in your legs flowing and prevent any clots forming.*

The day after your caesarean, you will be encouraged (after pain relief) to get up for a shower. You will have your catheter taken out first. Mobilising isn't usually as bad as people think, and the more you do it, the faster your recovery will be. Again – positive thinking!!

Your baby is safe, you are safe….. Let the fun begin.

CHECKLIST

Please don't feel a failure if you need help with the birth of your baby. The aim is a safe delivery.

Remember if you are given a date for a planned caesarean, then it may be postponed at the last minute, depending on what is happening on the delivery suite.

It is normal to have a lot of people in theatre. They all have their own job to do, and the team needs each one of them to function properly.

Decide before hand whether you are happy to have a student help to look after you, as a lot of hospitals are used to teach the next generation of midwives and Doctors.

If you are in bed for a while after having had an epidural or operative delivery, then remember to keep wiggling your feet and ankles to encourage good blood flow and reduce the risk of any blood clots.

Keep on top of your pain relief.

Chapter Fourteen

Your brand new baby

Your baby has been born (an achievement whichever way he or she decided to come out), your placenta has been delivered, and you have had stitches if you need them, your Midwife has gone to make you a cuppa, and your new born baby is lying safely in your arms. You've forgotten about the exhaustion, and this feeling has been replaced by elation. Enjoy this moment and take in everything.

If the lights are able to be dimmed, your baby will respond better. You wouldn't like a big torch shone in your eyes shortly after coming out of a dark room, so why would a baby?

You can then lie back and enjoy watching your baby being checked. The most important thing, especially if your baby is breast-feeding is for lots of skin to skin contact and as early a feed as possible. If baby is feeding, then this will take priority over weighing – something parents often ask literally as soon as baby is born - 'How much does my baby weigh?' I always smile at this as often they are still attached to their cord!

Once baby has finished feeding then he or she will be weighed.

DID YOU KNOW? *Nowadays, babies' weights are usually measured in kilograms. A lot of maternity units will probably have got rid of weight converters, as they can all be slightly different. The best weight converter can be found at the back of your baby's red book, and is probably the most accurate one.*

Your baby will two name bands put on, which will be checked with you, and have your surname on, even if you are not married and baby will be registered in a different surname. This is so that you and baby can be identified as being together.

It is really important that the two tags are kept securely on your baby at all times when you are in the hospital. Baby will usually have a security tag attached too, which will set off an alarm if baby leaves the ward. Tell a Midwife if one has fallen off, as it will need to be replaced as soon as possible. If both fall off, then every single baby in the maternity unit has to be checked to make sure they are with the correct Mum!

Your baby will then have an initial check by your Midwife, really to make sure there are no extra bits, or missing bits. Sometimes if your Midwife is trained to do it, the initial newborn examination will be completed too. This may be done later (by a Doctor if required), or when you get home. It needs to be completed by the time your baby is 72 hours old. This will check your baby more thoroughly, and make sure everything is as it should be, as well as listening to your baby's heart, checking for hip problems, and making sure the eyes are working properly. If any abnormalities are found, these will be discussed with you, and then your baby referred to a Doctor to see whether the problem needs extra investigation.

DID YOU KNOW? *When your baby's heart is listened to, then sometimes a murmur can be heard, especially if your baby is less than 24 hours old. Lots of changes need to happen to valves in the heart after birth. Sometimes the valves take their time to shut properly and a murmur can be heard.*

Any extra tests or scans will be arranged if needed, and your baby offered extra vaccinations if you have come from certain areas in the world, or have family living over there that may visit your baby. This is to reduce the risk of baby getting infected with conditions such as tuberculosis. The vaccination is called a 'BCG' vaccine. In certain situations, a hepatitis B vaccine may be offered.

Newborn babies can look a bit odd to begin with, as though they have been through a few rounds in a boxing ring:

Their eyes may look puffy and bruised
They may have a fine downy hair over their body, called 'LANUGO' – more so if they are early.
There may be some pressure or birth marks visible.
If your baby is of Asian, or a darker skinned origin, then a 'Mongolian blue spot' may be seen. These are blue coloured patches (they look like a bruise) and are commonly seen on the baby's back or buttocks.
Baby boy's testicles and baby girl's labia can be quite swollen and red straight after birth.

The first decision as a parent you will probably have to make (the first of many.....) is whether your baby is given vitamin K. Vitamin

K helps the blood to clot. All babies are born with low levels of vitamin K, and these stores get used up fairly quickly. In most babies they have enough stores to stop any bleeding, but a very small number don't have enough to make their blood clot.

It cannot be determined which babies will have a clotting problem. Due to this, vitamin K is recommended for all babies at birth.

As with anything, you can decline vitamin K, but most parents decide they will have it given to their baby. It can either be given as a one off injection (with a tiny needle – babies usually make more fuss about having their temperature taken!) or as a course of oral drops, the number dependent on whether you are breast or bottle feeding.

DID YOU KNOW? *Babies are not bathed routinely after birth anymore, as it can make them cold, and take away the protective properties on their skin.*

You may find your baby has a white creamy substance on their skin, usually in the creases and under their arms. This is called 'VERNIX'. Leave this on your baby's skin as it will reabsorb over time. If baby is early, then more vernix will be present.

Your baby will then have a nappy put on, and be dressed. Hopefully you will have packed an outfit in your labour bag, and baby can be dressed warmly in a vest, babygro, cardigan, hat and mittens.

TOP TIP! *Baby's cord will have a plastic clamp on it, so when you pop the nappy on,*

make sure the clamp is positioned outside of the nappy, so that it doesn't dig in to baby's skin.

Get your Midwife to show you how best to put the nappy on whilst the clamp is still there. A lot of midwives will now leave the clamp on until the cord falls off, so it may well be there for a week or so.

Dad's turn for cuddles now as when everything has been done to baby, then it's your turn!! If you are able to then you can get up and have a shower. If not then you will be offered a bed bath to freshen up. Clean pyjamas will never have felt so good!

DID YOU KNOW? *You will still have a fairly big bump after your baby has been born. This is normal and your tummy will flatten out over the next 6 weeks or so. Don't expect to jump straight back into size 10 skinny jeans – you may still need maternity wear for a few weeks. Breast-feeding helps to regain your shape quicker.*

Make sure when you are discharged from the maternity unit, you have;

Contact numbers if you have any concerns.
Your notes, red book and baby's cot card.
Any available information sheets.
Are confident with how to feed your baby.
Are aware of how to keep your baby safe when he or she is asleep.
Are aware of the plan of visits or appointments.

It is now your responsibility to strap your baby into their car seat, and ensure the car seat is fixed safely into your car, so make sure you know how to fit the car seat before baby arrives. On occasions I have seen people carrying the car seat into the maternity unit, still in its' box.

DID YOU KNOW? *Your baby's car seat should be rear facing, and put into the back of the car. If someone says to you 'Don't worry – I can turn my front air bag off, pop baby in the front', please don't. Air bags, even turned off can deploy in a crash and air bags and baby seats are not a great mix.*

TOP TIP! *If you are staying in hospital and have pets, then sometimes taking a muslin home that has baby's smell on it is a good plan. It will then help your pet adjust as the smell of your baby when they come home won't be as strange. Rub the muslin over them, so the baby's smell is intermingled into their scent.*

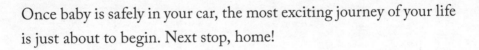

Once baby is safely in your car, the most exciting journey of your life is just about to begin. Next stop, home!

CHECKLIST

If possible, try and dim the lights in the room after your baby has been born.

Do as much skin to skin contact as you get to know your baby.

Feed your baby as soon as possible after birth.

Make sure your baby has 2 name bands on at all times when you are in hospital.

Come into hospital having made the decision as to whether you want your baby to have vitamin K, and if so, how you would like it given.

When you leave the maternity unit, make sure you have everything, including information leaflets, your notes, your red book and baby's cot card.

Double check before leaving that you know which numbers to ring if you have any worries when you get home.

Be aware of when your community Midwife will make the first visit.

When baby is in your car, double check the car seat is secured correctly and baby is rear facing.

If you have pets, have a muslin with you that has baby's smell on it, to make first introductions smoother.

Chapter Fifteen

Feeding

As feeding is the most important thing to master with a newborn baby, I am putting this chapter in first before I talk about tips for general baby care.

So many times I have done a visit and found a new Mum in tears saying she does not have 'enough' milk to feed her baby. This is one of the saddest things I hear.

As our society has evolved, we seem to have lost our faith in our body's ability. For 40 weeks your body has grown your baby, nourished it and kept it alive, so why would it give up on this precious new human after it has been born?

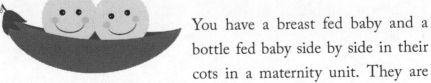

You have a breast fed baby and a bottle fed baby side by side in their cots in a maternity unit. They are both the same age, both the same sex and birth weight. You would think they would behave in exactly the same way, but they don't. If the reasons were explained to people, then maybe we could begin to believe in ourselves again.

It was for this reason alone I decided to write this book really. To try and get the lightbulb moment I see in new parents, when I sit down with them and it suddenly dawns on them WHY their baby is doing what it's doing.

I think, apart from seeing a new life enter the world (something that I marvel at every time I see it), my most rewarding aspect of my job is spending time with a new Mum and making her believe she can!

The next day I visit, I am often met with a completely different woman (and baby), and this is what I call it a 'lightbulb moment'.

A bottle fed baby, by the way it feeds, and how the milk is digested, takes a fairly big volume of milk in, and this milk lines the tummy making the baby full. The baby then has to sleep for a good period of time to digest the milk, and so quite quickly will get into a 3-4 hourly routine.

A breast fed baby functions in a completely different way. When a baby is born, it will have a breast feed (as soon as possible after birth preferably). This first milk is called colostrum and is high in fats, calories and important antibodies. This is the way you can provide your baby with a really special start in life by improving their immunity.

TOP TIP! Even if you really don't want to breast-feed, why not try and express your colostrum (it's there for about the first 2-3 days), and feed it to your baby in a bottle? The hospital can help you achieve this.

If everyone did this, who knows – our nation's health could improve in the future, and <u>you</u> would be the reason for that.

Because colostrum is so rich, and your baby will be worn out from the birth too, nature intends them only to feed minimally for the first 24 hours. This lets both of you rest, and as long as there are no medical reasons that your baby needs feeding more, you can both sleep.

Your baby may well sleep soundly for the first night. Make the most of it, as it won't last!

You will feel that your breasts are soft (another big worry of new Mums) for the first few days. You may not even see any milk leaking out, which again is completely normal. Don't worry – you will be providing milk for your baby, I promise.

On the second night, your baby will be up lots, maybe even feeding all night. This again is intended by nature as on day 3, your milk will 'come in'. You will not have any doubt then that you can feed your baby as your breasts will feel heavy and maybe leak. Your breasts may well feel huge at this stage. This will calm down as you and baby settle into a feeding routine. Love that cleavage for a little while.

TOP TIP! *Wear some breast pads and try not to express with a pump to relieve the full feeling. The breast is a delicate organ and will produce milk if stimulated. Your baby is the expert and knows when to feed and for how long. If you pump as well, your breast will think the baby needs more milk, and you will do the opposite of what you are trying to achieve – relief initially and then even more milk to deal with and even fuller breasts! This is why you need to get confident with hand expressing.*

Hand expressing

If you want to save the expressed breast milk, then have a clean, sterile container ready.

Hand expressing can also be helpful to encourage baby to feed in the first few days, or give baby some breast milk if baby isn't sucking very well.

Cup your breast with one hand, and then using your thumb and forefinger on your other hand make a 'C' shape about 2-3cm behind you nipple.

Gently squeeze and release in a rhythm until milk starts flowing. Move your fingers around the breast so all areas around the nipple are stimulated.

DID YOU KNOW? *Hand expressing shouldn't hurt. You may only see drops of milk coming out to begin with but this can be enough to encourage baby to latch.*

Storing breast milk (in a sealed, sterilised container)

At room temperature for 6 hours.

In the back of a fridge (not in the door) for up to 5 days, as long as the temperature is below 4 degrees Celcius.

In the ice compartment of a fridge for 2 weeks.

In a freezer for up to 6 months.

Once it is warmed to room temperature, then feed straight away and do not re-freeze or put back in the fridge.

DID YOU KNOW? *A cold savoy cabbage leaf (straight from the fridge) can do wonders for engorged breasts. They are kind of shaped like a bra, and maybe nature intended it to be that way for this very reason. Break off a leaf, get a knife and score on the inside of the leaf to*

125

let some juices and enzymes out, and then place inside your bra to ease any discomfort. Repeat as needed....

Parenthood teaches you patience, and the first lesson in patience will be the night feeds.

You will chat to your friend who is bottle feeding, and I can bet you she will say 'My baby sleeps so well. He only wakes up once a night and settles really quickly'. These are the worst words a breast-feeding Mum will ever hear. These are the words that cause the following feelings;

"I obviously don't have enough milk to satisfy my baby."

"I am starving my baby as he isn't settling at night."

"I am a useless mother."

"I need to top-up my 'failing' milk supply with formula."

As well as these feelings of doubt, the other worries creep in:

"As I can't see how much my baby is getting from my breast, it obviously isn't enough."

"I really need to see how much is going into my baby."

All of these worries are totally normal, and I want to change your way of thinking. When you do, you'll be so much more confident in your body.

The reassuring thing when bottle feeding a baby is that you have a full bottle, your baby drinks it, and then psychologically you feel satisfied. You know their tummy is full and your baby lies sleeping peacefully in their cot.

A breast fed baby will feed (a fraction of the amount a bottle fed baby will take in) and then quite quickly be hungry again. Their little tummies to begin with are the size of a marble, stretching slowly to the size of a walnut. This is because this is the way nature intended it. A breast will only make milk if told to by the baby feeding. What your baby takes, your body will remake, so you WILL have enough milk. A breast fed baby will take a small amount, quickly digest it, and then be back on the breast. It's very little and often feeding until your milk supply is established (and this can take 3-4 weeks).

DID YOU KNOW? *A breast fed baby does a few sucks, followed by a swallow. You will probably be able to see this. This means feeding is going well.*

Most people think of their breast in terms of a baby's bottle, with your nipple resembling the teat of the bottle.

Babies suck in two different ways, depending on whether they are bottle or breast-feeding. A bottle fed baby will latch on to the teat and use the muscles near the lips to feed. If you watch a bottle fed baby, then the lips will be drawn in as the baby compresses the teat.

If a breast fed baby tries to latch on to your nipple in the same way, then some milk will be drawn, but not very effectively. Therefore the baby will have to feed for a lot longer, and the end result will be a very sore nipple.

Although a nipple helps your baby feed by stimulating them to suck as it rests on the soft palate in their mouth, it isn't essential. If you have inverted nipples, then help is available for you to still be able to breast-feed. The areolar (the coloured part around the nipple) has all the important glands in it that your baby needs to compress to help your breast milk to come out. The nipple is really like the end of a funnel – somewhere for the milk to exit.

At the start of a feed, your milk will flow quickly and baby will get a large volume of milk, with lots of proteins and carbohydrates in it. This milk (foremilk) has relatively little fat in it. As the feed progresses, the volume of milk your baby gets will lessen, but the fat content will increase. This 'hind milk' will help your baby feel full up and sleepy.

Most babies use their hands to explore, which is lovely, but when you are trying to latch your baby on to the breast for the first few days, it may be easier to swaddle them for the initial latch.

TOP TIP! *Get a cotton blanket or sheet and lay in a diamond shape. Fold the top point down and lay your baby on the blanket with the baby's head above the fold, and the shoulders on the fold. Now place one of your baby's arms across their chest and wrap one side of the blanket across the baby, over their arm and tuck in. Repeat with the baby's other arm, so it is now on top of the first layer of blanket. Avoid using a fleece blanket as the baby may overheat.*

Once your baby is feeding, then loosen the blanket so your baby can get their hands out and explore. Babies will use their hands to help massage your breast and help the milk flow.

Breast-feeding may be uncomfortable for the first few days, but it should not hurt for the whole feed.

TOP TIP! *If the pain continues for more than 20–30 seconds, then pop a finger in the side of your baby's mouth to release their suck, and reposition baby.*

Much better to practice a good latch straight away than try and treat sore nipples. Babies learn by repetition – and they will soon learn a good latch gives them a better feed.

DID YOU KNOW? *When a baby is learning to feed, they can often be frantic at the smell of milk, and fuss at the breast, not really sure of what they need to do. Sometimes calming the baby by putting a clean little finger in the mouth (curled upwards) can get the sucking reflex started. If you do this with the baby near to the nipple, then a link is often formed with the fact the baby needs to actually suck!!*

You don't want an angry, distressed baby at the breast with both of you fighting each other, so get your partner, friend or family member to take them away from you for a few minutes. You'll find your baby is a little angel and will calm down and relax fairly quickly. You are then left feeling useless, a rubbish mother. The reason is – those other people don't smell of milk like you do. Yes they can settle your baby – but only YOU can feed your baby. So look at the positive always. You'll get your cuddle times very soon.

Babies will tell you they are ready for a feed in their own unique way. These are often referred to as 'feeding cues'. These include;

Making a 'smacking' sound with their lips,
Turning their head to the side and opening their mouth wide
Sucking on anything in sight

TOP TIP! *As soon as you baby starts showing these feeding cues, then the best thing to do is to pick your baby up before they start crying. Crying= 'You have IGNORED me and now I am going to show you how ANNOYED I am!'*

As with labour, breast-feeding is all about hormone let down. Hormones are needed to let your milk flow start. Therefore if you are stressed, that horrid thing called adrenaline will block the feeding hormones, as it did with labour. So you need a calm, relaxed baby at the start of a feed, so that you can relax too!

TOP TIP! *You may begin to settle in to a pattern, and feel smug. Babies have growth spurts, and a growth spurt = needing more milk. Therefore they will go through phases like they did just before your milk came in on day 3, and cluster feed to tell your breast to make more milk. This is a momentary blip. Again, understand why your baby is feeding more, and trust their instinct…. Your baby is the expert.*

DID YOU KNOW? *Breast fed babies don't usually need winding as due to the way they latch on, they don't take as much air in as a bottle fed baby. The end part of the feed will make baby appear sleepy, and so as baby comes off the breast, place down to sleep if possible.*

TOP TIP! *As well as reversing your sleep pattern for a bit, reverse your way of thinking for how much milk your baby has had. You won't be able to see what is going in but you will have a very good idea of what is coming out!*

Your baby should have 2-3 wet nappies in the first 48 hours and at least 6 wet nappies a day from day 5 onwards.

Your baby's poo should change colour from black to green to brown and then to yellow by day 4. It can sometimes look quite seedy too which is normal.

Your baby should have about 2 dirty nappies a day.

As soon as it gets dark, you relax for the evening, your adrenaline levels that have kept you going during the day will fall, and the hormones that make your long term milk supply will rise dramatically. Your baby knows this and it will be like a switch is turned on – WIDE AWAKE TIME!

This wide awake time usually happens for the first few weeks from dusk until dawn. This is normal. Swap your body clock around to suit your baby. Don't expect to be able to carry on as normal to begin with.

DID YOU KNOW? A breast-fed baby (of either sex) can get swollen nipples and a girl baby can have a bit of red spotting coming from her vagina. Both of these are due to hormones in the breast milk and are nothing to worry about.

Expect to be up all night to begin with, and the only way to cope with this is to sleep when your baby sleeps – in the day!

Most Dads have paternity leave for a few weeks. Make the most of it.

There is absolutely no point in both of you being up all night and not functioning. Work in shifts for a few weeks, and meet up for some together time in the evening.

A good routine…

1. Dad tucks you up in bed when he gets up in the morning after a good night's sleep.
2. He gets some quality time with baby. Lots of cuddles and changing of nappies! He also gets some time to look after

the house and do the essentials, so you don't have that added stress.

3. When baby shows signs of beginning to be hungry (fist sucking, mouthing and turning their head to the side), Dad can take babe in to you for a feed.

TOP TIP! *Respond to your baby's feeding cues BEFORE the crying starts. Once the baby is crying, it is fed up and feels ignored. A stressed baby will often fight at the breast, and in turn you will be stressed. This blocks the good hormones that let the milk down and the downward spiral has begun. Baby stressed = Mum stressed = baby more stressed = Mum even more stressed, and so on.*

4. If you want to stay in bed and feed lying on your side (which would be the ideal), Dad can stay watching baby in case you fall asleep feeding. Once the baby has fed, it's time for you to sleep and Dad to resume duties!

5. Try and have a meal together in the evening, and maybe any visitors (best to avoid loads of visitors in one go, and visits all day – they can sleep that night, you won't be able to) could come over for a few hours. Your baby will usually be nice and calm and alert at this time of day. Rested and playful prior to the night feeds.

6. When it is bedtime, now it's Dad's turn to have a good sleep to function the next day. Get yourself some snacks and drinks prepared and settle in for what is now your 'day'. Think of this as a really special time for you and baby to bond. There is no-one else around, just you and them.

7. Talk to your baby, look at every little bit of them, and expect the baby to be on and off feeding until it gets to dawn. <u>Enjoy</u>

this time – every parent will tell you they grow up fast, and they do, believe me.

8. If you expect to be awake and you know this is normal for the first few weeks, then you will be able to cope.

You cannot 'spoil' a newborn baby with love, cuddles and kisses. They don't know what spoilt is, and they won't have the connections in their brain yet to think 'Mmmmmmm.... if I cry, I will get what I want'.

They cry for a reason, either –

- They are hungry.
- They are in pain or poorly.
- They are tired.
- They are wet or dirty
- They miss you.
- They are bored.

They don't cry to manipulate – they may learn to as a toddler, but definitely not as a newborn baby, which is the stage this book covers.

Your newborn baby's cry is designed to make you feel stressed! If it didn't then you wouldn't attend to the baby's needs as quickly.

Sometimes Dads have a hard time adapting to breast-feeding. Many say they feel useless. First of all, successful breast-feeding happens with support – so they are a very important piece of the jigsaw. Secondly there are LOADS of ways Dads can bond with their baby – even nappy changing offers a chance to have lots of eye contact and closeness. Encourage Dad to have a bath with baby, do some gentle baby massage, do skin to skin contact.

Both be proud of yourselves as breast-feeding in the first few weeks of life offers many advantages to both you and baby. <u>These include:</u>

Protecting your baby's digestive system.

Providing your baby with immunity.

Clearing the sticky poo more quickly out of baby's system.

Providing milk at the right temperature.

Changing your milk to give baby what is needed.

There are even more advantages the longer you can breast-feed your baby. Such as reducing ear, gut, chest and urinary infections, eczema, asthma, childhood obesity and heart disease in later life. Breast-feeding has even been linked to higher IQ levels.

Breast-feeding is even great for you too as it helps your womb to contract after labour, so helping it return to its' normal size faster. It is free, readily available when out and about, reduces the risks of ovarian and breast cancer later in life, as well as making your bones stronger, which reduces the risk of brittle bones as you get older.

However, breast-feeding isn't for everyone. Yes it is the best option, but not at the expense of you hating it, dreading each feed, not enjoying your baby and getting low in mood. There always has to be choice in life, and as long as you are aware of the benefits of breast-milk, then you have every right to decide against it. A happy Mum = a happy baby.

DID YOU KNOW? *If you are having loads of issues breast-feeding, there are lots of support groups, help and advice available. Don't give it up if you haven't exhausted every avenue as you may well regret it..... It may well be as easy as changing the position you feed your baby in, or maybe using a nipple shield.*

Breast milk supplies can be replenished, but will take time to build up again, and depending on how long you have stopped for, may not get back to what it would have been.

DID YOU KNOW? *Sometimes babies have a favourite side to feed on. This may be because they have a sore head or neck from delivery. If they feed brilliantly on one breast, then trick them they are feeding on the same breast by sliding them around and tucking baby under your arm.*

TOP TIP! *If baby is unsettled, then maybe you could book an appointment with a chiropractor who specializes in newborn babies, to help realign their bones and relieve pressure areas.*

Talk to your Midwife about this if you are having problems.

Breast milk has lots of goodies in it that aren't just useful for feeding!!

Amazing things that breast milk does:

- *Use it to clean baby's eye if it is sticky.*
- *Wipe over baby's bottom if there are the beginning signs of nappy rash.*

Your Midwife will much prefer you to be honest about how you feel, and then you can be helped with your choice of feeding.

If you wish to bottle feed, then these days advice is different from when your parents made bottles for you.

For the first few days, your baby will only take 20-30 ml per feed, so the starter bottles are the best option until you have caught your breath and got organized. Believe me; even washing up a mug is a big event with a new baby.

If you can afford it, then there are machines that will prepare a bottle for you in minutes, ensuring it is at the optimum temperature.

However, bottles can still be made up in the traditional way, with a few adaptations.

<u>What you will need for bottle feeding</u>:

Bottles with teats and covers.
A bottle and teat brush.
Formula (powdered or ready to use).
Sterilising equipment.

<u>There are a few different ways you can sterilize your bottles, and these include</u>:

A cold-water steriliser.
A steam sterilizer.
Sterilisation by boiling.

(Sterilising equipment will be needed for breast milk expressing pumps and storing breast milk too).

STERILISING:

Wash your hands thoroughly with soap and water.

Clean your surfaces with hot soapy water.

Get your feeding equipment (they should be washed in hot soapy water with a bottle and teat brush as soon as possible after a feed, and then rinsed with clean cold water).

DID YOU KNOW? *Dishwashers will clean bottles, but not sterilize them as the water will not get hot enough.*

Babies immune systems is not as strong and developed as yours, so they are much more susceptible to infection and illness, which is why sterilization and good hygiene are vital to avoid issues like sickness and diarrhoea.

TOP TIP! *For all sterilising equipment, follow the manufacturer's instructions.*

Cold water sterilisers need the solution changing every 24 hours, and feeding equipment needs to be left submerged for 30 minutes before it can be used. Make sure there are no trapped air bubbles in the bottles or teats, as this means these areas won't be sterilized. Ensure all the equipment is kept under the water with a floating cover.

When using a steam sterilizer, make sure that the teats and bottles are facing down, so that the steam goes up into them when the water heats up. Timings are based on the steriliser, so check with you particular product. These sterilisers can be electric, or popped in the microwave.

If using boiling as your method to sterilize, then ensure your equipment is safe to boil, and keep it submerged for at least 10 minutes. Teats can perish quicker when this method is used, so keep a close eye on their condition.

MAKING UP A FEED:

Wash your hands and ensure surfaces are clean, as with sterilising.

Boil a kettle with at least one litre of FRESH non-boiled tap water. Don't reboil, don't use bottled water and seek advice if your house is fitted with a water softener.

Let the kettle cool slightly (for no more than 30 minutes) and use water above 70 degrees Celcius to make up the feed. This is to ensure that any bacteria that are present in the milk powder are killed off. This is rare, but can be life-threatening in a small number of cases.

Don't do what used to be done and put the water into bottles and leave in the fridge until a feed. The powder won't be exposed to a hot enough temperature to kill any rogue bacteria.

Get your sterilised bottle (shake off any excess solution if it has come out of a cold water steriliser) and stand on a clean surface.

Leave the teat, cap and retaining ring on the upturned lid of the steriliser, rather than on the kitchen surface.

Pour the water to the correct level in the bottle, and double check by getting down at eye level. Go with the manufacturer's guidelines on the milk powder tin.

Always put the milk powder in AFTER the water, or the formula will not be at the correct strength and may upset your baby's tummy or not provide them with the correct nourishment. Loosely fill the scoop and level off using a clean knife, or leveler which is provided in the tin. Only use the scoop provided in the tin as the manufacturers will have made sure that their scoop provides the correct amount of powder for a specified amount of water.

Hold the teat by the edge and place on top of the bottle. Then screw on the retaining ring without touching the end of the teat.

Pop the cap on over the teat, make sure it is secure, and give the bottle a good shake.

Make sure the formula is cooled down enough to feed by holding the bottom of the bottle and running it under a cold water tap. Keep the bottle moving so the milk swirls around and be careful not to let the tap water run over the cap.

Test the milk temperature by shaking a few drops onto your wrist. You shouldn't be able to feel it either hot or cold.

DID YOU KNOW? *After a feed, throw any remaining milk away. Don't feed the milk to your baby if it is over two hours old (from when it was made up) and never re-warm in a microwave as it can heat the milk unevenly and hot spots can be present which may burn your baby's mouth.*

Made up bottles with powdered milk must be made up as you need them. They must not be stored in the fridge, so the days have gone where 24 hours of bottles could be made in one go. Well-meaning older relatives and friends may try and convince you that this is absolute rubbish, but guidelines are there for a reason, and the risks have been researched.

Ready to use formula milk CAN be stored in the fridge. The fridge must be clean and the carton stored, with the flaps turned down, at the top of the fridge, towards the back if possible. They can be stored for 24 hours once opened.

TOP TIP! *When you are out and about with a bottle fed baby, I would advise taking a couple of empty sterilised bottles out in a bottle cooler bag. Take a small carton of ready to use milk and a clean pair of scissors. When baby is ready for a feed, the milk can be divided between a few bottles and won't have been hanging around. The bottle that hasn't been drunk can be kept cool and used for the next feed – you will just need to ask for a jug of hot water to bring it up to body temperature.*

If you have to use powder, then take the required number of scoops with you in a clean container, a flask of fresh water that has just been boiled and a sterilized empty bottle. Don't forget to cool the feed down as you will be making it up when the baby needs a feed.

When you are bottle feeding your baby, maintain good eye contact with your baby. This will make them feel loved and secure. Feed your baby skin to skin whenever possible, with a blanket covering you both. Dad can do both of these things too. Try for the first few weeks to give the feeds yourselves, to help develop a close bond.

Pop a bib or muslin under baby's chin and hold baby slightly upright when feeding; making sure their head is supported. Brush baby's mouth with the teat as you would do with your nipple and 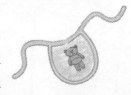 allow baby to open their mouth wide and draw the teat in. Your baby will tell you when they have had enough, so don't try and force them to take in more milk than they want to, unless they are on a feeding plan and need to take in a certain amount of milk. Even then, don't force the issue, but phone the maternity unit or your community Midwife for advice.

 Take regular breaks and allow baby to bring up any wind. You don't need to bang the baby's back for hours. If they haven't burped after about 30 seconds, then they probably haven't got any wind to bring up. Often just sitting the baby upright is enough to shift any wind.

When baby has finished feeding, make sure the creases in their neck are clean and free from dribbled milk, which if left there may cause bacteria to multiply.

Bottle fed babies should be having wet and dirty nappies like a breast-fed baby does, however their poo may be slightly more formed.

Sometimes (as with trainer cups – I went through about 30 different cups before I found one that didn't leak and my son approved of!), you may have to try different types of bottles. Some babies struggle with teat designs, maybe due to the shape of their jaw, and you will find one particular design suits baby better.

This also goes with colic too. Colic can be a problem with a newborn baby, but anti-colic bottles are available – often with a special straw system which reduces the amount of air a baby takes in per feed. Colic can be recognized by your baby drawing their legs up to their tummy when they are crying.

Discuss feeding issues with your Midwife before buying. As with breast-feeding, often problems can be easily sorted. This includes starting to use infant colic products too.

TOP TIP! *Only feed a newborn baby with first (or stage one) infant milk. If they are hungry, increase the amount of feed you give them rather than switching to hungry baby milk. Hungry baby milk is designed more to help delay weaning. Any concerns with whether you are feeding the correct milk, then speak to your Midwife or Health Visitor. This applies to switching to specialist milks too, which are often obtained by prescription, or feeding cooled boiled water.*

DID YOU KNOW? *If your bottle fed baby is suffering with constipation, then sometimes feeding them the ready-made milk for 24 hours, rather than powdered milk can often sort the problem out.*

CHECKLIST

Remember a breast fed and bottle fed baby feed completely differently.

Think seriously about giving your baby your colostrum, even if you aren't keen on breast-feeding.

Babies normally sleep for a long period after delivery. If they have had a good feed, use this time to catch up on sleep.

Soft breasts in the first few days are normal and it doesn't mean you don't have any milk.

Stock up on a savoy cabbage and keep in the fridge.

Breast fed babies are designed to feed at night and sleep during the day to begin with.

Reverse your body clock to suit your baby, not the other way around.

Remember you see what is going into a bottle fed baby. With a breast fed baby, have confidence they are feeding well by what is coming out in the nappy!

Breast fed babies feed little and often. Stay calm and relaxed when breast feeding. Sleep when your baby sleeps – housework can wait.

If breast feeding hurts, then reposition your baby. Get baby to latch properly from the beginning. It is easier and less painful to avoid sore nipples, than it is to treat them.

It's normal if you are breastfeeding not to be able to settle your baby due to the smell of your milk.

Dads have a massive role to play even if they cannot physically feed baby.

Be aware of the other uses for breast milk.

Be aware of how to sterilize bottle feeding equipment, making up feeds and storage times if you are bottle feeding.

Dishwashers' clean bottles, but they still need sterilizing before use.

Only store ready-made milk, not made up powdered milk in the fridge.

Remember lots of eye contact when feeding.

Having a special box of toys is often helpful to amuse your toddler at feeding time.

Chapter Sixteen

The first week at home with baby

The first few days and weeks at home with a new baby can be daunting. I hope this book will have helped you through pregnancy and birth, and now help you to become a confident parent.

A Midwife will look after you and your baby for at least the first 10 days of life. Depending on your hospital's policy, the day your baby is born is counted as day 0.

Visits (or hospital clinic appointments) will vary, but are usually:

The day after you come home for your first visit.
Baby weight on day 2-3.
Baby weight, heel prick test and to check your stitches or caesarean wound on day 5.
A discharge visit on day 10.

DID YOU KNOW? A Midwife will rarely give you an exact time for a visit. This is because the workload may change if there is an emergency, or a visit taking longer than planned due to an issue with a Mum or baby.

Please make sure you are at home for your visits, as each visit will be for a reason. You will get days when you won't have a visit, so best to plan trips out on these days. In the early days rest is more important.

Baby's sleeping environment

Remember your baby has come from a warm, noisy, cramped space – your uterus grows with your baby, so they have always had a feeling of being secure.

We then put them in a Moses basket, in a quiet room and expect them to sleep. It must be very frightening for them, which is why they will settle as soon as you hold them and cuddle them to your chest. They feel held, warm and can hear the one thing that is so familiar to them - a heartbeat.

One of the first worries you will have is having the courage to sleep at night when baby sleeps. For the first few nights it is tempting to sit up watching your baby to make sure he or she is still breathing. Babies are survivors and ensuring they are safe in their sleeping area, will reduce the risk of what was called 'Cot Death'. This is now referred to as 'Sudden Unexplained Infant Death Syndrome' to stop parents thinking that the only place their baby could die was in their cot. Other risk factors will be discussed next.

DID YOU KNOW? *Babies are safest in their Moses basket to sleep.*

If you wish to bed share, then seek the advice of your Midwife before you leave the hospital. With bed-sharing, you are subjecting the baby to all of the things we say avoid when placing them in their Moses basket. Bed sharing is not advised if you have had alcohol to drink, taken drugs (which include sleep remedies), are exhausted or smoke.

If you wish to bed share, then do everything possible to prevent your baby from getting too hot, suffocating or getting stuck.

Your mattress has to be fairly firm and the bed positioned so that baby cannot fall out or get trapped between the mattress and wall.

Keep the room temperature between 16 – 18 degrees Celcius.

Dress baby in bed clothes that resemble what you would wear in bed. Be very careful not to let baby overheat.

Ensure your bed covers can't overheat, or smother your baby.

Always supervise your baby. Don't leave them alone in or on your bed at any time.

Make your partner aware you are taking baby to bed with you.

Avoid sleeping an older sibling next to baby – there should be an adult between the older child and baby.

Keep pets out of the room.

There are certain reasons why a baby can be more at risk of sudden infant death. These are:

Over-heating your baby.

Exposing your baby to smoke.

Positioning your baby incorrectly in their bed.

Letting your baby share their bed with soft toys or pets.

Using duvets, pillows and bumpers.

The best ways to keep your baby safe are:

Keeping the room temperature between 16-20 degrees Celcius (18 degrees being the best temperature) – you do not have to replicate the temperature of the maternity unit, which is designed for very new and premature babies. A healthy term baby will be able to regulate their body temperature more successfully after 24 hours old.

Ensuring you do not overheat your baby. A baby's hands and feet will remain blue and cold for quite a while, as their blood is needed where their main organs are. Check baby's temperature by feeling inside the back of their baby gro. You will soon feel whether the baby feels too hot or cold.

The general rule is a baby needs one layer extra to what you are comfortable in. Remember if you fold a blanket in half, then that will be two layers. Fold that blanket in half again and that will be four layers. Easily forgotten when trying to make a blanket fit into a small Moses basket.

Avoid using fleece blankets as they can overheat your baby. Cotton, hand-knitted or cellular blankets are best.

Avoid duvets and pillows too, as they can increase the risk of suffocation.

Be careful with gro-bags – check if it is a gro-bag suitable for a newborn baby, as quite a few specify that the baby needs to be over 10 lbs in weight.

Avoid placing baby's crib next to a fire, radiator, and heater or in direct sunlight and don't put an electric blanket or hot water bottle in the Moses basket with baby.

Lay your baby on his or her back with feet right at the bottom of their bed to ensure baby can't pull the blanket over their head.

As lovely as cuddly toys are, best not to have any cuddly toys in with baby as they can grab them and pull in front of their faces, increasing their risk of suffocation.

Make sure the family cat cannot cuddle in and sleep with baby. Invest in a cat net, or make sure your furry friend cannot enter the room at night that baby is sleeping in.

Keep baby in your room for the first six months.

Make sure you do not fall asleep on the sofa with you baby, or in a chair. Babies can wriggle, and sofa cushions have suffocated babies.

If you have to smoke (and I highly recommend you try really hard to give up), then you must smoke outside and mustn't cuddle baby for at least 2 hours after a cigarette. Advice has gone away from changing your top, washing your hands and brushing your teeth. Cigarette smoke can be exhaled for a long time after you have finished your cigarette and if you are cuddling your baby, then any smoky breath may be inhaled by your baby, which is the same as a baby passively smoking. The same applies to not having a cigarette just before you go to bed as the room will be filled with exhaled fumes, and as baby is sleeping in your room, they will be at risk.

If baby appears unwell, then seek medical advice quicker than you would do for yourself. Your Midwife will make you aware of emergency contact numbers, and these are usually written in the front of baby's red book too.

Sudden infant death can occur in car seats too. Make sure baby isn't overheated, and isn't in their car seat for long periods. I would say after an hour a baby should be taken out and allowed to stretch. Don't be tempted to leave baby in the car seat when you get home. Take baby out as soon as possible and pop them in their Moses basket.

TOP TIP! *Be aware of your baby's environment in the car. A newborn baby venturing out will need to be kept warm, but as baby gets a little older, then on a cold day remember not to bundle baby up, then take your coat off and turn the heating to full blast. The same applies to air conditioning in the summer. Be aware of your precious bundle in the back who can't tell you they are too hot or cold. Don't forget the sunshades too and something for baby to look at as they tend to get a bit bored with looking at the back seat for a long time!*

Dummies

Try not to use a dummy to begin with for a breast fed baby as they need to be on the breast regularly, rather than sucking on a dummy. If you do introduce a dummy, it is recommended that you offer your baby a dummy EVERY time you put baby down to have a sleep. If  baby spits the dummy out, then it's not a problem, but it can slightly increase the risk of sudden infant death if your baby has got used to going to sleep with a dummy and one isn't given.

Pets

Family pets can feel jealous if shut out, if they normally are allowed in the house with you. Often this can start problems as the pet becomes jealous of this new 'thing' that has suddenly moved in and taken over. In my opinion it is far better to try and adjust your pet to your baby, as long as baby is safe. When you bring baby home, if you haven't done the muslin smell trick, then take the blanket in first that baby has been wrapped in and let the animal sniff the blanket. Give them lots of fuss before you bring baby in. When baby comes in, leave the baby in the car seat so that your pet can sniff baby at a safe distance. Again, makes lots of fuss of them before getting baby out of the car seat.

When you do hold baby, then make sure one of you gives your pet attention. Maybe have your dog on a lead to begin with until they get used to their new housemate.

If your pet is aggressive, or very easily stressed then it may be worth investing in some time with a pet behaviourist when you find out you are pregnant, as although family pets are important, your baby's safety is top priority.

Checks that need to be done:

WEIGHT

Your baby will be weighed at birth, and then depending on your hospital's policy, on day 2 or 3 and days 5 and 10. Other weights may be needed if there are any concerns.

DID YOU KNOW? *More than likely your baby WILL lose weight to begin with. Don't panic and think that you're a bad mother or get upset. A drop of 10% is normal in the first few days. Your baby will have probably done enough poo to fill a lot of nappies (the sticky first poo that looks like tar), and will have had to use calories to keep warm, feed and adapt to moving in a water-free environment. So if your baby's birthweight was 3000g, then a drop in weight to 2700g is fine. In pounds and ounces this can sound quite scary, but if your Midwife isn't worried then neither should you be.*

NEWBORN BLOOD SPOT TEST

This is a test that is offered between days 5-9, and is usually done as close as possible to day 5, and at the time of writing this book tests for nine conditions that although they are very rare, can cause your baby to have serious health problems. The sooner they are picked up and treated, the better your baby's long term health will be.

Find out if any member of your family have (or are carriers of):

- Sickle cell disease.
- Cystic fibrosis.
- Been born with a low thyroxine level.
- Any metabolic conditions.

If they do, then let your Midwife know as soon as possible as this will have to be noted on the form that your baby's blood test is sent off on.

Your Midwife will explain the procedure, what the test is for and get your consent. If you are happy then a small device will be used to prick your baby's heel. Four good sized drops of blood will be collected on a special card made of blotting paper.

TOP TIP! *Let your baby suck on something to take their mind off the test. There are two schools of thought on whether you should feed your baby at the same time as the test in case they associate the pain with later feeds. In my experience feeding them doesn't seem to be a problem, and is a good way to do the test. However, your Midwife may have a different thought, so take the advice of whoever is taking the test.*

The new devices are a lot more effective at getting a good drop of blood out of your baby's foot, but this can be helped by popping some socks on your baby's feet on the morning of the test. Warm feet = a better blood supply.

Sometimes your Midwife may need to repeat your baby's blood test later on. This doesn't mean your baby has a problem. It may be that there is not enough blood (which is more common now that more conditions are being tested for), the card with the blood on has become damaged or lost, or has been contaminated.

You don't have to agree to your baby having the test, but I would highly recommend it as it could save your baby's life.

You can have the test done when you baby is older (up to 12 months old), but cystic fibrosis can only be screened for up until 8 weeks of age. The reason the test is done early is so that conditions can be picked up and treated as early as possible.

DID YOU KNOW? *No news is good news as the lab will only report urgently on positive results, or those that need re-testing.*

Eventually the results will filter through to your GP, and be available to your Health Visitor by the time your baby is about 6-8 weeks old. The results will be recorded in your baby's red book.

Nappy changes

You may have heard the phrase 'top and tail' referred to. This basically just means a freshen up and nappy change.

Get everything you need ready. <u>This includes</u>:

2 different coloured bowls (one for the face and one for the bum) – remember which one is which as you wouldn't wash your face in toilet water!
Cotton wool

TOP TIP! *Avoid using wipes and creams on a newborn baby when at all possible. Use cotton wool and warm water to avoid baby getting sore.*

Changing mat
Towel or absorbent pad
Clean nappy
Nappy bag
Hand sanitiser

Put a towel, or absorbent pad on to the changing mat to keep baby warm, and soak up any spillages!

Get out a nappy bag and open up ready for dirty cotton wool etc.

Get all your bits ready – 2 pots with warm water, cotton wool, clean nappy.

Pop baby on the towel and if you are going to top and tail, clean baby's face first before changing the nappy. With one piece of damp cotton wool, clean one half of the face, avoiding the eye area. Dry with clean cotton wool.

Repeat with a new bit of damp cotton on the other side of the face and dry.

Clean under the chin area with a new bit of damp cotton wool and dry well.

Undo the bottom half of baby's clothes and tuck up behind baby so the nappy is clear of clothing.

Undo the nappy and wipe any excess poo away with the inside front of the nappy, and fold under baby, so baby's bum is now laid on the outside of the nappy, and any poo etc. safely inside.

Now clean baby with cotton wool and warm water. Girl babies need wiping from the front to the back when cleaning.

TOP TIP! *Boy babies will wee as soon as you take their nappy off as fresh air hits a certain part of their anatomy. Take the nappy off, but keep the nappy over until you are certain a wee isn't coming!*

DID YOU KNOW? *If you want your baby boy to have some fresh air time without a nappy, pop a sock over your little boy's private parts. If they wee, then it won't create a huge fountain as the sock will absorb it.*

Remove dirty folded nappy and ensure baby's entire bottom is clean and dry with dry cotton wool.

Lift baby's legs up and pop a clean nappy underneath. Make sure the back of the nappy is positioned a nice distance up baby's back.

After fastening the nappy (you should be able to fit a finger in comfortably between the nappy and baby's tummy), make sure the cord is positioned outside of the nappy, and all the ruffles around the legs are pulled out to stop any soreness or leakage. Clean your hands before picking up baby.

TOP TIP! *Do not be tempted to use creams on a baby to prevent nappy rash. Modern disposable nappies are designed with lots of micro holes in them to draw the wee away into the nappy and not sit against baby's skin. Cream blocks these holes and can have the opposite effect.*

DID YOU KNOW? *If your baby does have the beginnings of nappy rash, try cleaning their bottom with a weak cooled chamomile tea solution. If you are breast-feeding, express some breast milk onto a cotton wool pad and wipe baby's bottom with your breast milk. The main thing is lots of fresh air. Seek medical advice if the soreness does not heal, or it is spreading. Try and catch in good time. Creams may then be needed, but only if advised.*

TOP TIP: *If you are using eco-friendly bio degradable nappies, make sure you have the bio degradable nappy bags, or all the good you are trying to achieve will be undone.*

You could save a lot of money by investing in washable nappies. There are loads of choices available, and some companies offer a nappy washing service too.

Bathing baby

Try and leave baby for as long as possible without having a bath. You can clean the creases in their skin with warm water and cotton wool. When you do bath baby, you don't need a load of gadgets, just a new washing up bowl to begin with, or popping them in a warm bath with you. If you do this then make sure the water is warm, rather than hot, and you aren't using any perfumed bath products. Obviously if you are really dirty, then re-plan!!

TOP TIP: *Bathing baby in the sink in a new washing up bowl is a great way to gain confidence to begin with, and means that if you have had a caesarean, then you don't have to kneel down or bend forwards.*

<u>So How DO I bath my baby?</u>

Get everything ready and to hand. <u>You will need</u>:
Changing mat
Cotton wool
A baby sponge
2 clean towels
Fresh nappy
Fresh clothes
Some baby shampoo
A bowl or baby bath

Get baby's bath water ready and at the right temperature (test with you elbow, and as with milk, it shouldn't feel too hot or too cold. To begin with don't put any products in.

Now undress baby, but leave the nappy on.

Wrap baby in a towel, with arms and legs tucked in, and the only visible thing being baby's head.

If you are right handed, tuck baby under your left arm and support baby's head with your left hand (vice versa for you lefties!!).

Dampen baby's hair down using the bath water, with a little sponge or your hands.

Apply a tiny amount of baby shampoo and massage in.

DID YOU KNOW? *Babies have two soft spots on their head, the main one being a diamond shaped area at the top of their head, the other being a small triangle shaped area at the back of their head, just above the neck. Eventually these will close over as the skull grows, but be careful to begin with not to press on them.*

Rinse baby's hair and dry gently with either another small towel, or the hood of a hooded towel.

Now take the nappy off, and clean baby if dirty.

Get a clean towel laid out and lie baby in the crook of your left hand (opposite arm if you are left handed), and hold the top of baby's left arm with your left hand. Lift baby up supporting the bottom with your free hand and sit baby down in the water. Baby will be nice and safe as the head will be supported by you forearm and won't slip as you have hold of their arm.

With your free hand then just gently splosh water over baby's body to keep baby warm. As you get more confident then you can swap hands and sit baby forwards. To begin with though, just let baby kick and enjoy.

Lift baby out and wrap up in the dry towel. Pat dry, rather than rubbing the delicate skin. Pop on a clean nappy and fresh clothes. Pop a cardigan on to make sure baby is kept warm and give them a nice cuddle, taking in that lovely smell of a freshly bathed baby.

Playtime

Your newborn baby will LOVE interaction with you. This will help develop their brains and cement a lasting bond.

Good ideas for playing with your baby include:

Interact with your baby when they are awake (but you don't have to do this constantly! – if they are awake and content, then you leave baby to absorb their new environment).

Lots of cuddles – skin to skin if possible.

Smile and chat to your baby, ensuring good eye contact.

Keep the Moses basket near the centre of the home activity so baby feels included.

Carry your baby around in a sling, enabling new outlook on the world – make sure the baby's neck is well supported.

Give your baby black and white patterns to look at. They love them and will help their eyes develop.

TOP TIP! A newborn baby won't be able to see more than the distance from the crook of your arm to your face for the first few weeks. Place toys near enough for them to see. Interact with them at a distance they can recognize you.

Tummy time

Tummy time is great at helping your baby develop their neck muscles, which are really important for when they start sitting up and crawling later on, and promotes a more rounded head shape.

Try and carry it out as often as possible when baby is awake. Good ideas for helping your newborn get some 'tummy time' is to lay baby either on your chest, over your shoulder or over your forearm.

Keeping your baby safe

Keep baby safe by preventing accidents. Even a young baby will like to put things in their mouth as this is how they learn about their environment – especially if the colours are bold and eye-catching.

Be especially careful about putting a nappy bag near baby when it's changing time. Especially if you set everything out, lie baby on a change mat and then remember you have forgotten something. Your baby could grab the nappy bag and pull over their face.

CHECKLIST

When at home, please try and stay in until your Midwife has visited.

Rest in the first few weeks – there will be plenty of time to be out and about when you have found your feet.

Babies are designed to be cuddled and close to you – you can't 'spoil' a newborn baby.

Remember not to overheat your baby.

Baby's environment needs to be smoke free – that means no cuddling for 2 hours after a cigarette.

Check baby's temperature by feeling inside the neck of their Babygro.

Remember a baby's hands and feet are naturally blue and cold to start with.

Keep your home between 16 – 20 degrees Celcius. 18 degrees is the best temperature for a baby.

Avoid using fleece blankets, duvets or pillows when baby is sleeping.

A Moses basket is safer in the early days with just baby and blankets – no cuddly toys, unless they are out of reach.

A baby's weight will naturally drop by up to 10% in the first few days.

Remember to get prepared before you do a nappy change or bath baby.

Try to avoid using wipes, creams or products on a newborn baby's skin if possible.

Don't forget about the healing properties of breast milk.

Emma Cook

Play and interact with your baby as often as possible when they are awake, but let baby have some time to take in their new surroundings too.

Keep baby safe.

Chapter Seventeen

What about you?

Becoming a mother (or parent) equals immense emotional and physical challenges, however much you have prepared for your baby,

or are supported by your family. As I said earlier in this book, the media portrays motherhood as being blissful and easy. This can then put pressure on to you when you feel it should be like this and it isn't.

Your body may well still be recovering from your birth, and you may feel sore. Hopefully you will have stocked up on some of the things mentioned in Chapter nine. Taking Arnica early can help reduce the pain of bruising, and keeping up with your pain relief. If your pain is controlled then this can help you emotionally too.

You may feel 'cheated' if birth didn't go quite as planned, but I hope after reading this book you may have changed your view.

Your body will still resemble being pregnant, and this is normal. Your tummy won't be like an ironing board straight after delivery. It can take weeks if not months to return to the same shape you were before you became pregnant.

Stretch marks may still be visible. Think of these as your baby wounds – be proud of what your body has achieved.

TOP TIP! *Instead of your pain being like a wave, try and alternate your paracetamol and ibuprofen, under the guidance of your Midwife. Make sure you do not exceed the recommended doses, and double check the strength of ibuprofen that you are taking.*

If the area that you are sitting on is sore, why not try some homemade ice packs? Clean the surfaces of your kitchen and lay out 6-8 maternity pads. Boil a kettle of clean water and in a jug put some freshly boiled water, along with a few drops of tea tree and lavender oil. Dampen the pads with the mixture (they don't need to be soaking!), and pop them in a clean plastic bag and put them in the freezer. You can then take a pad out every few hours and use it as a clean maternity pad/ice pack.

TOP TIP! *If it stings when you wee because of grazes, or stitches, try sitting on the toilet facing the cistern, or have a wee in the bath or when taking a shower!*

Try and keep your stitches clean and dry. Change your pad regularly and allow air to get to that area where possible. Bacteria love warm, moist environments, so keep everything dry and they will find another home.

Visitors

Visitors can wait! Your baby will still be small enough for them to see in a few weeks. These few weeks are all about you. If you don't want to get dressed, then don't. If you want to sleep, then go to bed. If you're hungry, eat. Listen to your body and take its advice.

TOP TIP! *Partners make great 'gate keepers'. Minimise visitors to start with to very close family and friends – and even then they have to either bring a casserole, or take on some ironing! They are not the one's left with a tired baby who has been passed around. They will go home to bed!*

TOP TIP! *Offered help? Then take it! Friends and family members are a great source of helping with housework, cooking meals and generally being your slave. Don't feel guilty – if they offer, then make the most of it!*

DID YOU KNOW? *Dirty dishes and dust don't matter in the first few weeks. Your Midwife will be more worried if you are up, dressed, full make-up on and house immaculate, than if you look disheveled and surrounded by a little bit of chaos!*

Postnatal blood loss

Most maternity units will give you an information sheet at discharge to highlight what is normal blood loss, and when you need to seek advice. Don't forget, as with pregnancy and babies, every woman will be different.

Postnatal blood loss is often heavier during or following a breast-feed due to an increase in hormone levels making your womb contract. You may not feel any pain, but just notice an increase in blood loss after a feed, or your loss becoming redder in colour.

You will also notice that you blood loss may slow down and then start to increase as you feel better and do more. However your blood loss should still stay the same colour, rather than becoming bright red.

DID YOU KNOW? *Postnatal blood loss smells quite metallic. It has a distinctive smell, which is normal. It's not horrid, but should be checked out if the smell changes and becomes offensive.*

What to expect:

Day 1

A fairly heavy red or reddy brown loss that soaks a maternity pad in about 2 hours.

Day 2-6

Your loss will become a darker red, pinky red or brown. The amount on your pad should be decreasing, from a 4 inch stain, to a 2 inch stain.

Day 7-10

Blood loss should be reducing and getting lighter in colour. It may become heavier again if you are more active.

Day 11-14

Continuing to get lighter. May be a pinky-red now when you are more active. Some pads may not have anything on them.

Weeks 3-6

May well continue as a brown-pink colour, or paler.

DID YOU KNOW? *If your loss stops after 2–3 weeks and then returns again around week 4–6, then this may be your first period (if you are not breast-feeding).*

Blood clots

During the first few days after birth, you could pass a few large clots, about the size of a satsuma. Some women pass smaller ones. If you are worried, save the clot for your Midwife to see. Usually if your blood loss is slow after a clot is passed, then better out than in.

TOP TIP! *Seek medical advice if your blood loss soaks a maternity pad in less than 30 minutes, or remains heavy after a clot has been passed.*

DID YOU KNOW? *It is not usual to keep passing large clots after the first few days. Any worries then contact your Midwife, or GP.*

After pains

These are cramps that can vary from mild period-type pains to pain similar to that of contractions in labour. These are less common after a first baby, but the more babies you have, the more likely you are to get them! They do improve after a few days, but can take around a week to stop. Take regular pain relief.

If your pain changes or you don't think it is due to after pains, it may be due to a womb infection, urine infection or constipation. Sometimes the pain can be combined with feeling shivery and unwell, and an increase in blood loss or an offensive smell. If any of these symptoms occur, then contact your Midwife or GP as you may need antibiotics.

Mastitis

This is caused by an infected milk duct that has usually become blocked. It is different from the engorgement you feel when your milk comes in. Mastitis is often seen as a red band on part of your breast, along with pain and the feeling of having flu.

The best remedy is to keep feeding baby and massage the area where the redness is towards the nipple to help free any blockage.

DID YOU KNOW? *Placing baby's chin in line with the red area can more effectively unblock that milk duct.*

Pop baby on a pillow and kneel over baby on the bed. Encourage baby to latch on with the chin touching the area that is red – you may have to get yourself in an odd position, but it can really help.

If the problem persists and you feel poorly, then ask your Midwife or GP for advice as you may need to have a course of antibiotics.

Baby blues

These commonly occur around day 3-4 postnatal. The baby blues are linked with tiredness, breast-milk coming in and baby becoming more demanding prior to your milk coming in. It is very transient and normal. You will cry at anything, and these feelings will usually disappear within a few weeks.

Postnatal depression

A small percentage of women will get postnatal depression, and it will usually be someone close to you that notices a problem. It can occur in the first year after birth. Depression is less of a taboo subject these days, but can still be difficult to admit to.

TOP TIP! *Think of depression as a broken brain – you would need treatment for a broken arm and your brain is just the same. It just needs help and it isn't your fault. Brains, as with arms, can be fixed. It is VERY treatable.*

TOP TIP! *If you suffered with postnatal depression with a previous baby, then make sure your Midwife is aware early on in the pregnancy. Sometimes medication can be given to prevent it happening again and your Midwife and GP will be able to keep a closer eye on you.*

<u>Your loved one may notice that:</u>

You are becoming increasingly tired.

You are irritable, anxious or panicky.

You have mood swings.

You are tearful or distressed.

You are having trouble sleeping.

You have trouble remembering things.

You have a poor appetite.

You have lost interest in things that you used to enjoy doing.

You become distanced from your loved ones.

You become detached from your baby.

You become angry about your life now.

You show a lack of eye contact.

You feel you are a 'bad' mother.

You have a complete drop in your confidence.

Your thoughts become obsessive and fears are exaggerated.

TOP TIP! *(For loved ones) – don't say 'Snap out of it' or 'Pull yourself together' – as this will make the matter worse, as will compound the feelings of usefulness.*

If any of the symptoms are present, then it is best to see your GP as soon as possible for advice and treatment. Your Midwife will extend your postnatal visits and listen to your worries. Other health professionals will be informed so they can support you too.

If you get help, then help leads to help, and you will realise you are not alone in your feelings.

There are lots of support groups out there, and therapies that are not just medication related – these include counselling, hypnosis, aromatherapy, massage, alternative therapies. Maybe even a short stay in a specialized mother and baby unit may be recommended if you are really struggling.

I had very bad postnatal depression for about 2 years. The reason why I say please talk to someone is because it took me a long time to admit I wasn't coping. I remember sitting in a meeting at work with my team and announcing that I couldn't do on-calls as I couldn't go on a dual carriageway. I then burst into tears and they realized I needed help. I felt that being a Midwife, I should be able to cope and so I hid it.

It started off with worrying about my baby's safety to it snowballing in to agoraphobia. I started off avoiding dual carriageways as I felt that my car would crash and my baby would be at risk. It then snowballed into not liking roads with hedges in case anything happened (as I wouldn't be able to stop). I then became terrified of being in an area that was isolated, and eventually didn't want to leave my house.

I eventually opened up to my team as I felt safe with them. It had got to the point where I was finding travelling to visits in my car a problem, and it was a case of 'Tell someone, get help, or lose the job I love'.

The relief was immense. I saw my GP, got help and had hypnotherapy. I could have avoided 2 years of hell if I had been honest. Please learn from my mistake. The silly thing was that I was helping lots of women who were feeling the same as me, and I couldn't see it in me. This is why it is often your partner or a close person in your life who will notice it first.

If you have thoughts that are out of touch with reality, and this has developed quickly, then this may be a very rare condition called 'Puerperal Psychosis'. This is a psychiatric EMERGENCY and will usually require admission to hospital.

<u>Puerperal Psychosis signs include:</u>

Severe fluctuation in mood.

Severe agitation.

Ideas that include 'Being famous', 'Being extremely wealthy', 'Being extremely powerful, or able to do things that wouldn't normally be possible'.

Confusion.

Fear.

Poor concentration.

Sleeping issues.

Becoming violent.

Disorientated about what time, day or year it is.

Poor insight.

Hallucinations.

Rapid or slurred speech.

Suicidal thoughts.

The good news is that, as with postnatal depression, it is usually easily treated and you will respond well with a few weeks of treatment starting. Often symptoms have disappeared after 6-8 weeks and you will feel back to your normal self

You wouldn't ignore a lump, so don't ignore signs of being mentally unwell.

<u>Other symptoms that require urgent medical attention:</u>

<u>**Pre-ecalmpsia**</u> can occur after your baby has been born, even if you have had no problems during your pregnancy. So get checked if you have any signs of a severe headache combined with:

Visual changes, and/or
Nausea, and/or
Vomiting.

<u>**Pain, swelling or redness in the back of your calf muscle in your leg.**</u>
<u>**Difficulty breathing.**</u>
<u>**Chest pain.**</u>

<u>Your pelvic floor muscles</u>

To help healing and prevent problems later on such as leaking wee when you are bouncing on the trampoline with you 4 year old, then be vigilant about doing your pelvic floor exercises.

Your pelvic floor muscles support your bladder, bowel, womb and vagina. They control when you wee or have your bowels open and can be weakened during pregnancy and childbirth.

Weak muscles can lead to leaking of urine, reduced control of your bowel and a lack of sensation during sex.

So how do you exercise them?

Choose a comfy position and put your knees slightly apart.

Tighten up your back passage like you would if you were trying to stop wind coming out.

Hold these muscles and at the same time tighten the muscles you would use to stop yourself from having a wee.

Do each time you feed baby so you remember, and aim to do 4 slow 'squeezes' and 4 fast 'squeezes' per feed.

CHECKLIST

If you don't find motherhood easy to begin with, it is quite normal.

You will still look pregnant for a while after your baby has been born.

Take regular pain relief.

Think about taking arnica as soon as possible.

Make ice packs in case you need them.

Keep your stitches as clean and as dry as possible.

Ration visitors at first.

Accept any offers of help.

Save any large clots for your Midwife to see.

Seek medical advice early if you think you may have an infection.

Try and feed through mastitis, and try massaging your breast where the sore area is and try different feeding positions.

Crying is quite normal, but seek help if it carries on for more than the first few weeks.

Postnatal depression is nothing to feel embarrassed about. Seek help as soon as possible as it can be treated effectively.

Seek urgent medical help if you have any warning signs, such as a severe headache, visual disturbances, pain, heat or redness in your calf muscle in your lower leg, have problems breathing or chest pain.

Remember to do your pelvic floor exercises every time you feed your baby.

Chapter Eighteen

When do I need to worry?

Babies are designed to worry you. As soon as you find out about your pregnancy, the worry starts, and believe me, it doesn't end. As our parents still worry about us, so you will continue to worry about your baby. The worries change as they grow, but what things with a newborn baby need to be checked?

Common concerns with a newborn baby:

Jaundice (yellowing of the skin or eyes) after 24 hours of age.
Nappy rash.
Thrush.
Constipation.
Diarrhoea.
Crying.
Colic.
Wind.
Skin issues.

A lot of these common complaints, such as nappy rash, constipation, crying, colic and wind have been discussed earlier in the book, so please refer to these conditions in Chapters 15 and 16.

Jaundice

When a baby is in your womb, they get the leftovers of the oxygen you breathe in and don't need, so they become expert at being able to grab the oxygen. They can do this as they have loads of red blood cells in their blood to make use of every possible bit of oxygen.

When baby is born and breathing its own air, then these extra red blood cells aren't needed, so the baby's liver starts to break them down. It is sometimes a mammoth task for the baby's liver to do, and sometimes there is a byproduct called bilirubin left over when the red blood cells are broken down. This substance is what turns baby's skin and sometimes eyes yellow.

If the jaundice appears after 24 hours of age, and your baby is term and well, then babies usually sort themselves out without medical intervention.

The main things to do is to help your baby get rid of the bilirubin by making sure their system is flushed through with plenty of fluid and they are weeing regularly. If baby is alert, waking for feeds and feeding regularly, the Midwife will just keep a close eye.

If baby shows signs of:

Being unusually sleepy,
Not feeding,
Having dry nappies.

…Then you should alert your Midwife or maternity hospital as soon as possible.

DID YOU KNOW? *Jaundiced babies are sometimes treated by being placed under an ultraviolet light in hospital. A mildly jaundiced baby can benefit not only from regular feeding, but to be placed in natural (not direct) light.*

Thrush

Often seen as a thick white coating on the baby's tongue, which is still there an hour or so after a feed and not easily removed with scraping. This needs treatment as it can be sore. If you are breast-feeding, the thrush can get into your nipple and cross infect baby and you, so you will both need treatment.

Contact your Midwife if you are worried, and a prescription can be arranged from your GP, in the form of oral drops for baby and nipple cream for you.

It can also cause nappy rash too. Also be vigilant when bottle feeding or using a dummy that these are washed and sterilized thoroughly to get rid of any thrush on the silicone.

Diarrhoea

Seek advice if baby appears unwell, or if not feeding very well. Don't forget a breast fed baby's poo will be more liquid than a bottle fed baby's poo, as there is less waste with breast milk.

Rashes

Babies start off looking beautiful with blemish free, perfect skin, then they can resemble a teenager! Often you may well see a rash that looks like acne or a mosquito bite and moves around your baby's body. This is often quite normal if your baby appears well, and will resolve after about two weeks, but if you are worried then contact your Midwife.

Tiny white or yellow spots, called 'milk spots' can appear on your baby's face or body and are again quite normal. These spots are usually seen grouped together.

Baby can get a small red pin prick looking heat rash if overheated, so if you notice this then make sure you strip layers off your baby to cool them down.

Most rashes are fine. I will discuss the more worrying rashes in the next section.

Emergencies that need urgent attention:

Jaundice before 24 hours of age.

If jaundice is present in your baby before they are 24 hours old, this may indicate a problem that needs urgent medical attention. There may be a problem with your baby's liver or a blockage in the bile duct and will need reviewing by a Doctor as soon as you notice it.

No meconium passed within 24 hours of birth.

This will need an urgent review too in case your baby's bottom does not have a proper opening. It can also be linked to other possible conditions. However it may just be that baby has passed meconium in your womb, and is delayed because of that reason. It still should be checked out though.

Some rashes.

Meningitis is the obvious emergency. Make sure you are aware of how to perform the 'glass test'. Press a glass over the spots and if they do not disappear then this may be a sign of this serious condition. Get the baby to a hospital immediately.

Fever.

A normal temperature for a newborn baby is between 36.5 – 37.2 degrees Celcius. If baby's temperature rises over 38 degrees Celcius, this could indicate infection, especially if you have had risk factors in pregnancy, such as group B streptococcus, a fever in labour, or your waters were broken for over 24 hours.

Floppy/ limp baby.

A healthy term baby should respond when picked up, and have good tone in their muscles. If your baby is floppy or limp when you pick baby up, then get the baby straight into hospital.

Breathing issues.

Most newborn babies can be quite snorty and snuffly; however they should not be making a huge effort to breathe. If you notice your baby is puffing their nostrils out, breathing really rapidly, making a 'grunting' sound or sucking their chest in when they breathe, then this could indicate a serious problem. Seek medical advice as soon as possible.

CHECKLIST

Check out jaundice if:

It appears before your baby is 24 hours old.

If baby is not feeding well.

If baby's nappies are dry.

If baby is unusually sleepy.

Be aware to seek urgent advice if your baby has not had a poo within 24 hours of birth.

A fever of over 38 degrees Celcius could indicate an infection.

A floppy, limp baby is not normal.

Problems breathing need urgent medical attention.

If in doubt, seek medical advice.

Chapter Nineteen

Life without your Midwife

If everything is OK, then your Midwife's last visit will be around day 10. Often the Midwife who has looked after you for the pregnancy will try and do you discharge visit, so it may be slightly after day 10, depending on their Rota. This will depend on each hospital's policies too.

When the Midwife discharges you, then baby will be approaching, back to or over their birthweight – remember babies lose weight to begin with, and this is normal.

Your next best friend will be your Health Visitor, who will normally see you shortly after your baby is 10 days old. Sometimes these visits overlap with your Midwife, but don't worry.

Your health visitor will then see you through the next phases, such as baby's hearing test and developmental checks, immunisations, longer term feeding, growth, weaning etc. and are there to give you advice as you need it with any worries such as potty training and sleep patterns.

When your Midwife does your last visit, she will check as to whether a Health Visitor has been in touch, and arrange a visit if one isn't in the pipeline. The Midwife will also check that you have remembered to register your baby, don't have any lingering worries and are aware of contraception.

DID YOU KNOW? *Even really effective breast-feeding doesn't ensure you won't get pregnant again, so be prepared if you don't want your children in the same school year!*

If you are breast-feeding, then you won't be able to take the contraceptive pill that has oestrogen in it. The mini-pill (or progesterone only pill) is fine. Check with your GP if you want to restart the pill, as they can often be started again on day 21 postnatal. You can then obtain a prescription. Other methods (except condoms) have to be sorted later, so book an appointment to discuss your choices, such as the coil, depot injection or implant at around about 6 weeks postnatal.

I hope you have enjoyed this book. I have tried to include everything I would chat about in my day to day life as a Midwife, which is why I called this book 'A Midwife in My Pocket'. I hope it will make the most exciting journey of your life enjoyable, rather than stressful. This book is meant to compliment the care you receive from your own maternity unit, and is designed to simplify things, so that you can delve deeper if you need to in more comprehensive books.

I take a great deal of pride in helping the women, babies and families in my care, and I thank them for giving me the courage to do this.

Most importantly, remember every one of us are unique, and every pregnancy is different. Life would be boring if we were all the same. Rather than worrying because you friend's pregnancy is different to yours, look inside yourself and use your instincts. If it doesn't feel right, then it probably isn't. Get it checked!

My advice for life – especially one with a new baby in it....... Have a great big filter attached to your ears as EVERYONE from your family members to a passing stranger will have a view on how you should bring up your baby.

The best approach is to agree politely (which will result in less tension or prolonged conversation), and then file the information you think will be useful in your brain and ditch the rest!

Thank you for taking the time to read my book, and I wish you all the luck in the world on the amazing journey you are embarking on.

About the Author

I have been a midwife since 1999 and trained in Hampshire. I have worked for the majority of my career in the community. My home now is in Dorset.

It was an honor in 2014 to win a national award. One of the student midwives whom I guided through her training nominated me for this award. I was amazed to be short-listed. Being the actual winner of the Midwives Magazine Mentor of the Year was inspiring.

I feel passionately about caring for the families I look after, and I find imparting my knowledge to the next generation of midwives a privilege.

Living in an extended family enables me to have the joy of returning from work to be greeted by my four-legged friends and my very special son. He takes my job in his stride, and I delivered most of his classmates! He always reminds me to take care if I have to go out to a birth in the middle of the night.

The greatest joy in life is becoming a parent. Being a midwife is the next best thing.

Printed in the United States
By Bookmasters